UPLIFTED

Maximizing Your Potential through the Triumphs of Black Women

ZARA TRACE

TABLE OF CONTENTS

Why I wrote this book..7

The Spark Before the Fire: Ancient African Queens and Matriarchs..........9

Matriarchal Majesty: The Powerhouses of Ancient Africa 12

Queendoms of Old: Societies Where Women Ruled.......................... 15

Crown and Scepter: The Regal Influence of Queen Mothers 18

Mystics and Oracles: Women in the Spiritual Fabric of Africa 20

Shieldmaidens and Strategists: Warrior Women Shaping Africa........ 23

Legends of Yesteryear: Celebrating Nefertiti, Amina, and Asantewaa
.... 25

Echoes of the Ancestors: How Ancient Matriarchs Mold Us Today 28

Roots Reclaimed: The Inspirational Legacy of Our Foremothers 31

Soulful Heritage: Exploring the Spiritual Depth of Black Womanhood 33

Ancestral Echoes: Unearthing Our Spiritual Foundations 36

Spiritual Melting Pot: The Diaspora's Tapestry of Faiths 39

Empowerment Through Faith: The Spiritual Strength of Black
Women 42

Healing Hands: The Restorative Power of Spiritual Practices 45

Wisdom Across Ages: The Sacred Teachings of Our Elders 48

Artistic Revolution: Claiming Identity Through Creativity....................... 51

The Canvas of Our Lives: Arts, Identity, and Empowerment 54

Sculpting Resilience: Visual Arts as Tools of Expression 57

Words of Power: Literature as a Reflection of the Black Female Soul
.... 60

Rhythms of Resistance: The Cultural Celebration of Music and Dance
.... 63

Creative Fire: Modern Artists Changing the Narrative 66

Voices of Change: Black Women Leading the Charge in Justice................. 69

Marching Through Time: Pioneers in the Fight for Equality............. 72

Breaking Barriers: Black Women's Political Journeys 75

Fists in the Air: The Firebrands of Black Power and Feminism 78

The New Guard: Today's Movements Shaping Tomorrow 81

Unbreakable Bonds: The Power and Importance of Community................*84*

The Role of Community in the Lives of Black Women.................... 87

Sisterhood Unbreakable: Circles of Support and Empowerment 90

Gullah/Geechee: A Legacy of Resilience and Unity 93

Healing Circles: Traditional and Modern Restorative Practices 96

Grassroots Glory: Black Women Spearheading Change 99

Bridging Generations: The Power of Mentorship 102

Together We Rise: Building Stronger Communities 105

Legacy of Triumph: Overcoming Adversity Together *107*

Passing Down Resilience: Lessons From Our Elders 110

Standing Tall: Stories of Courage and Victory 113

Forward Ever: Black Women Paving the Way................................. 116

Seeds for Tomorrow: Cultivating Hope and Strength...................... 119

Reclaiming Our Narratives: The Power of Our Stories............................*122*

Reflections on the Past: Examining the Strength and Resilience of
Ancestors 125

Reclaiming History: Learning from the Stories and Achievements of
Unsung Heroines 128

Nurturing Future Leaders: Cultivating Empowerment, Knowledge,
and Self-Expression in the Next Generation 131

Owning Our Strengths: Embracing the Unique Talents and
Contributions of Black Women 134

Passing the Torch: Empowering Young Black Women Through
Mentorship and Support 137

Creating a New Narrative: The Importance of Storytelling and
Sharing Personal Experiences.. 140

Building a Better Future: Harnessing the Power of Community and
Collaboration to Shape the Legacy of Black Women.......................... 143

The Empowered Roots Movement: Redefining the Narrative of Black Women *146*

The Movement Redefined: A New Chapter Begins 149

Breaking the Mold: New Perspectives on Black Womanhood 152

Leading Lights: Profiles in Courage and Innovation 155

Digital Diaspora: Social Media Shaping Our Stories 158

Tomorrow's Trailblazers: Nurturing Young Black Minds 161

Changing the Game: Education and Media's Role in Transformation 164

Unity in Diversity: Expanding the Circle of Inclusion 166

Looking Forward: The Evolution of Our Movement 168

A Celebration of Us: Honoring the Journey of Black Women *171*

Reflecting on Resilience: The Unbreakable Spirit of Black Women 174

Unlocking Potential: The Role of Support in Fostering Success 177

Intergenerational Wisdom: The Gifts of Our Ancestors 180

Leading from Every Angle: Black Women as Multidimensional Leaders 183

Sisterhood Stronger Together: Fostering Connections for a United Future 186

WHY I WROTE THIS BOOK

In a world where the narratives of Black women often unfold in the margins of history, my journey to pen "Uplifted" was ignited by a profound desire to cast a spotlight on the indomitable spirit, enduring wisdom, and cultural richness of Black women through the ages. This book is more than just a compilation of historical facts; it is a heartfelt tribute to the legacy of strength, resilience, and unparalleled contributions of Black women to the fabric of societies across the globe.

My motivation stems from a personal yearning to bridge the gap between the past and the present, to reconnect our generation with the ancient African matriarchs whose leadership, wisdom, and spiritual depth laid the foundational stones of civilizations. These women, often unsung heroes of their time, wielded power and influence that shaped the course of history, yet their stories have been overshadowed by narratives that fail to acknowledge their significance.

As I delved into research, I was moved by the countless tales of Black women who, despite facing insurmountable odds, rose to lead resistance movements, pioneered innovations in science and the arts, and nurtured communities through times of turmoil. Their unwavering courage and the rich tapestry of their experiences compelled me to share their stories, to ensure that their voices are heard, their achievements celebrated, and their wisdom passed down to future generations.

This book is an ode to the spiritual fortitude and cultural heritage of Black women. It celebrates their role as custodians of knowledge, bearers of tradition, and architects of society. From the ancient queens of Africa to the modern-day heroines marching on the front lines of change, their legacy is a beacon of hope and empowerment for Black women today. It is a testament to the fact that the spirit of the Black woman, resilient and undiminished, continues to inspire, challenge, and uplift.

Writing "Uplifted" was also a journey of personal growth. It challenged me to confront my own understanding of history, to question the narratives that have been traditionally upheld, and to embrace a more inclusive and nuanced perspective. This book is an invitation to readers to embark on this journey of discovery and reflection, to explore the depths of a history that is rich with lessons of endurance, leadership, and the power of collective action.

My hope is that "Uplifted" serves as a source of inspiration and empowerment for all readers, especially Black women. I wish for it to be a reminder of the strength that lies within our shared heritage, a call to recognize and honor the contributions of Black women throughout history, and a beacon of encouragement for the continued fight for justice and equality.

"Uplifted" is more than just my contribution to the annals of history. It is a declaration of love and respect for the enduring spirit of Black women. It is my way of saying, "Your stories matter. Your voices are powerful. Your legacy is undying." Let this book be a mirror reflecting the true essence of Black womanhood, in all its glory and complexity, for generations to come.

THE SPARK BEFORE THE FIRE: ANCIENT AFRICAN QUEENS AND MATRIARCHS

Ethnographic studies of pre-colonial African societies have shown that in numerous communities, women played critical roles in governance, religious practices, and economic activities. This was prevalent in the Kongo and Dahomey Kingdoms, where women held positions not only as queens and queen mothers, but also as priests, traders, and military strategists, which showcased the importance of the equal distribution of power and the respect given to women by the society.

The role of queen mothers in ancient African societies cannot be understated. They wielded significant influence within their respective kingdoms, often serving as trusted advisors to their children and community leaders. Queen mothers carried the lineage, inheritance, and the right to the throne, and in this way, they ensured the preservation of their kingdom's heritage. Their wisdom and strength were greatly cherished, often positioning them to be key decision-makers in political, social, and economic matters.

One such queen mother was Yaa Asantewaa of the Ashanti Empire, who led her people in resistance against British colonial rule in the early 1900s. Yaa Asantewaa demonstrated the resilience of ancient African matriarchs by using her knowledge of military strategy and her unwavering determination to defend her people's way of life against foreign oppression. Her story serves as a testament to the exceptional strength of the women that came before her and the power of a unified community.

Another facet reflecting the resilience of ancient African matriarchs is the role of powerful priestesses in spiritual life. Women were significant contributors to religious practices and spiritual beliefs in pre-colonial African societies, often serving as spiritual leaders, healers, and mediators between the people and their deities. The veneration and respect accorded to these women laid the groundwork for future generations of black women to embody a deep sense of spiritual connection and resilience.

The Yoruba goddess Oya, for example, is worshipped as the powerful deity of transformation and change. According to traditions, she governs the gates between life and death, and it is she who ensures that life's changes—both good and bad—are met with resilience and strength. Today's black women invoke her power and wisdom as they navigate myriad challenges in life, using their faith as a source of inner strength and solace.

Ancient African matriarchs also displayed their resilience by serving as skilled warriors and military strategists in times of conflict. One of Africa's most celebrated female warriors, Queen Amina of Zazzau, led her people in military campaigns and conquests across West Africa in the 16th century. She expanded the kingdom's territory and fortified its defenses, instilling a deep sense of pride and resolve among her people.

Today's black women look to these examples, as well as countless others, to inspire their own fight for social justice in contemporary society. The resilient spirit of ancient African matriarchs has been passed down through the generations, continuing to provide strength and wisdom for black women in the current day.

In conclusion, the foundations of resilience are grounded in the stories and experiences of ancient African matriarchs whose wisdom, spirituality, and determination have persisted through time. Black women today continue to draw upon the strength of their ancestors, constantly redefining and augmenting the legacy of these resilient women. By understanding and appreciating the roots of this resilience, black women and their descendants can continue to forge new paths and shape their own resilient narrative, further adding brilliance to the kaleidoscope of black women's histories. As we move to the next section of this book, it is paramount for readers to keep in mind the invaluable lessons passed on by our forbearers and seek to preserve the essence of resilience that has characterized their lives and our own.

Matriarchal Majesty: The Powerhouses of Ancient Africa

In the tapestry of human history, the thread of ancient African matriarchs weaves through its fabric in rich hues of wisdom, strength, and resilience. As one delves into the tapestry's intricate patterns, one cannot help but be struck by the profound significance of the roles these women played in their societies. Hailing from empires and kingdoms scattered across the African continent, these matriarchs laid the foundation for the very essence of Black womanhood, carving out a legacy that continues to inspire and empower generations of Black women today.

The importance of these female figures in the pre-colonial African context can be gleaned from the various roles they occupied in their communities. Far from being confined to the margins of society, ancient African matriarchs were known to wield considerable power and influence, occupying key positions within their respective polities. They shaped the course of history as rulers, queen mothers, spiritual leaders, warriors, and strategists—each role imbuing them with a unique set of qualities and competencies that would ultimately pave the way for the achievements and triumphs of their descendants.

As leaders of their people, these ancient matriarchs presided over their realms with the wisdom and discernment honed by their experiences, sagacity passed down through generations in a rich tradition of oral history. They were not merely figureheads; their rule was characterized by their ability to broker alliances, build political networks, and manage the machinery of governance effectively. Some, like the Candace of Meroë, were known to be political trailblazers; she led her armies into battle against the Romans, boldly confronting the might of one of the most powerful empires in human history.

In their roles as queen mothers, these ancient African matriarchs played the essential function of guardians of their people's cultural heritage. Bearing the responsibility for the transmission of knowledge, traditions, and customs to future generations, they enjoyed a singular kind of reverence in their communities. It was through the stewardship of these queen mothers that the ancient African kingdoms maintained their ties to the past while navigating the ever-changing landscape of the present.

Perhaps most striking of all was the role of ancient African matriarchs in religious matters. As spiritual leaders and priests, they served as conduits connecting the realms of the seen and the unseen. These women were held in high esteem, their authority stemming from the belief that they possessed a unique ability to communicate with the gods and goddesses, interceding on behalf of their people in times of need. In their counsel, ancient African communities found solace, guidance, and hope.

Beyond their spiritual roles, these matriarchs also wielded great martial prowess. Defiant in the face of adversity, they led armies into battle, inspiring awe and admiration in friend and foe alike. Whether clad in the regalia of a warrior-queen like Amina of Zazzau or garbed in the spirit of resistance like Yaa Asantewaa of the Ashanti Empire, they were the embodiment of courage and determination. Their indomitable spirit, inherited by generations that came after them, epitomizes the essence of resilience that is the hallmark of the Black woman.

As we embark on this exploration of the lives and legacies of ancient African matriarchs, it is crucial to bear in mind the multifaceted roles they played in their respective societies. Each stood as a testament to strength, resilience, and wisdom--values that continue to reverberate through the collective consciousness of Black women today. Their stories serve as both compass and guide, pointing the way forward as we trace the colors, contours, and shades of our ancestral lineage. In their footsteps, we find uncharted possibilities, picking up the threads they spun and weaving them into our own story—bold and resplendent.

Queendoms of Old: Societies Where Women Ruled

The ancient world was a tableau of contrasts, a rich mosaic where matriarchal and patriarchal societies coexisted. Given the duality of these contrasting social orders, Africa was no exception. Tracing our fingers along the trajectory of its evolution, we encounter societies where women stood at the helm, cultivating and nurturing the ethereal essence of the land. Among them were the Akan people in West Africa, the Kikuyu in East Africa, and the Kongo Dynasty in Central Africa. The women from these societies, our ancestors, carved their marks in stone, creating a lasting legacy that continues to resonate with us. The cultural impact of these early African matriarchal societies offers a glimpse into a world where the power dynamics lay in the hands of women, who shaped the fabric of their communities in profound and enduring ways.

Let us journey back to the era of the Akan people, who established their presence in parts of modern-day Ghana and Ivory Coast. The Akan social order was steeped in the sacred tradition of matrilineal inheritance, tracing the bloodlines of individuals through their mothers. This uniquely empowered women as the custodians of land and property, as well as the bearers of their lineage, ensuring the intergenerational transmission of the tribe's customs and knowledge. Within this matrix of power, the queen mother was the most pivotal figure, respected and revered for her wisdom. Functioning as a spiritual leader and a mediator in the political arena, the queen mother's influence wove the social fabric together, facilitating cohesion and stability.

The Kikuyu people of East Africa were yet another bastion of the matriarchal order. Residing in the verdant highlands of modern-day Kenya, the Kikuyu women held sway over the community's resources by being directly responsible for agriculture. In this capacity, they exhibited considerable authority in the allocation of land, enshrining their importance as the community's economic linchpin. Their role also extended to the transmission of cultural identity, as it was through their songs, dances, and narratives that their people stayed connected to their ancestral heritage.

The Kongo Dynasty of Central Africa presents us with another sophisticated portrait of matriarchal society. The Kongo Kingdom flourished along the banks of the Congo River, in present-day Angola and the Democratic Republic of Congo. Forming the backbone of their matrilineal social structure were the women who, as in the Akan society, wielded immense authority in the realms of land ownership and succession of power. The Kongolese queen mothers similarly presided as esteemed spiritual leaders, bringing harmony and blessings to their people in both the physical and metaphysical worlds.

Each of these African societies was distinguished by the unique ways in which their women shaped and influenced the cultural landscape. Far from being passive bystanders, they actively contributed to the development and growth of their communities through their roles as custodians of material wealth, transmitters of cultural heritage, and spiritual shepherds. In the process, they ensured the continuity of their civilizations, leaving an indelible mark on the hallowed ground of history.

As we delve into the cultural impact of these early African matriarchal societies, it is crucial to recognize that their legacy lives on in palpable ways. Contemporary feminist scholars and African diaspora activists continue to draw inspiration from the traditions and practices exemplified by these ancient matriarchs, as a counter-narrative to the often-traumatizing cultural legacies of patriarchy and colonialism. Their incredible stories offer a crucial window into an alternative social order that centered on women, celebrating their agency, wisdom, and resilience. They hold within them the seeds of rebirth and rejuvenation that future generations can harness in their journey toward healing and empowerment.

As we embark on the next voyage into the ancient world of Africa's queen mothers, spiritual guides, and warriors, we take with us the rich wisdom of our forbearers, their strength, and their indomitable spirit. In the songs and stories borne on the wings of the wind, among the whispers of ancestors long gone, lies the sacred tapestry of our collective narrative. For it is in the footsteps of these ancient matriarchs that we continue to tread, reaching back across time to grasp the threads they wove, fashioning ourselves in their image, and rekindling the flame that they once ignited. With each bridge we traverse, we enshrine their legacy in our hearts and minds, forging a radiant and powerful connection to the timeless essence of Black womanhood.

Crown and Scepter: The Regal Influence of Queen Mothers

One such figure is that of Nana Yaa Asantewaa, queen mother of the Ashanti Empire in present-day Ghana, who commanded unyielding respect for her valor and courage. In the early 20th century, under her leadership, the Asante people fiercely resisted British colonial rule. As the king and other leaders had been exiled, Yaa Asantewaa assumed the mantle of military leader, rallying her troops and harnessing their resolve in the face of adversity. Though the war ultimately resulted in British victory, Nana Yaa Asantewaa's bravery bolstered the morale of her people, inspiring them to hold fast to their cultural identity despite the external onslaught.

Across the continent, in the Kingdom of Matamba of Angola, we encounter another remarkable ruler – Queen Nzinga, who deftly maneuvered her way through the treacherous landscape of 17th-century African geopolitics. Confronted with the threats of European colonialism and the burgeoning slave trade, Nzinga deftly leveraged her diplomatic prowess to negotiate and form alliances with both domestic and international powers. Through this delicate balancing act, she managed to maintain her kingdom's sovereignty, even in the face of military defeats. Queen Nzinga's shrewd political acumen, combined with her remarkable grasp of both European and African customs, enabled her to skillfully maintain her state's stability and protect her people from the ravages of external forces.

From the Horn of Africa, a unique figure in the pantheon of African female rulers emerges. Queen Gudit, who ruled in the 10th century over the Kingdom of Damot (now part of modern-day Ethiopia), is remembered for her unyielding determination to topple the ancient Aksumite Empire. Her successful campaign not only brought about the end of this long-standing power, but it also ushered in a period of resurgence for the once-subjugated people of Damot. As a revolutionary force, Queen Gudit embodies the notion that a single determined individual can forever reshape the trajectory of a region's history.

One cannot discuss African queens without acknowledging the indomitable Hatshepsut of ancient Egypt. As one of the few female pharaohs, Hatshepsut crafted a reign that advanced Egypt's fortunes through trade, diplomacy, and grand architectural projects. Under her rule, the kingdom thrived, and her influence reverberates through centuries of Egyptian history. Although attempts were made to erase her contributions from the historical record, evidence remains of her impact on Egypt as a prosperous and secure nation.

The legacies of these African queen mothers are intricately woven into the continent's rich historical tapestry. Their leadership elevated the empires they ruled not simply by their ability to command armies or consolidate territory, but also by their foresight and understanding of the intricate political machinations required to navigate a complex global landscape. As stewards of their people's welfare and guardians of their culture, the decisions they made influenced not just the lives of their contemporaries but also the generations that followed.

In examining the lives and legacies of these legendary African queen mothers, we are reminded that the resilience, wisdom, and courage they embodied remain an indelible part of the collective identity of Black women today. As we forge ahead into an uncertain future, the examples set by these ancient matriarchs serve as beacons, guiding us with the knowledge that the qualities they displayed--strength, sagacity, adaptability, and determination--are as relevant today as they were centuries ago. As we carry their memories with us, we proudly stand on the shoulders of these giants, threading the vibrant colors of their legacies into the fabric of our futures. As we continue to unravel the stories and histories that make up our collective past, let us find solace in the strength of our ancestors and the visionary women who shaped the destinies of the empires they ruled. In this legacy, we too can find the courage to envision groundbreaking pathways, forge powerful alliances, and harness the unrivaled potential within ourselves to create a future worthy of those who came before us.

Mystics and Oracles: Women in the Spiritual Fabric of Africa

As we venture further into the annals of ancient African history, canyons and chasms of time are bridged, revealing a cultural tapestry woven with powerful stories of spirituality and the eminent roles of women as priestesses. The sacred history of African priestesses unearths not just the roots of our people's beliefs and rituals, but also the undeniable influence of women as guardians and intercessors of the spiritual realm. In the ancient African world, where spirituality was not simply a matter of abstract metaphysics but a vital, elemental force coursing through every aspect of daily life, women emerged as the preeminent conduits of the divine, harnessing the supernatural to shape the destinies of their people.

For the ancient Africans, spirituality transcended the boundaries of rigid dogma, blossoming instead into an experiential lifescape that seamlessly merged the natural and the metaphysical. Women, in their roles as priestesses, were the vital linchpins in this cosmic dance, bridging the realm of the spirits and the mundane world through ceremonies, rituals, and initiation rites. Their unique status within their communities endowed them with the singular capacity to commune with the spirits, beseeching blessings and guidance for their people and interceding on their behalf in times of tribulation. As custodians of this sacred connectivity, their influence was not only manifest in the religious sphere but also heavily permeated the social, political, and cultural fabric of their societies.

One prominent example of the potency of the female spiritual leaders is gleaned from the ancient civilization of Nubia, specifically, the Kingdom of Meroe, nestled between present-day Sudan and Egypt. Here, the High Priestess of the Kushite god Amun held sway over the most sacrosanct temple, assuming the mantle of divinity for her kingdom. The Priestess, La Mrey Reo, was renowned for her ability to interpret oracular messages and omens, and wielded considerable authority in the realm of both spiritual and temporal affairs. She presided over the court assemblies and ceremonies as the earthly manifestation of the celestial beings, influencing decisions, and determining the course of events.

The spiritual heritage of West Africa is similarly infused with the power of the female priestesses. At the heart of the Yoruba civilization lies the Ifá divination system, a complex process of communing with the spirits to seek wisdom and guidance through the intercession of the priestess. The Iyanifa, the High Priestess of Ifá, was not only a repository of the oral tradition, preserving the knowledge of sacred texts and esoteric wisdom but also served as a conduit between the spirits and the Yoruba people. Her astute interpretation of divinations shaped and influenced the destiny of the community, weaving a nuanced, syncretic relationship between the mortal and transcendental worlds.

A journey to the southern tip of Africa, among the Xhosa people, brings us closer to the essence of the female spiritual leader through the figure of the Sangoma or the traditional healer. The Sangoma holds a position of immense respect within the Xhosa community, mediating the cosmological balance between ancestral spirits, the living, and the land itself. Through her spiritual gifts and ancestral connection, she diagnoses and heals spiritual ailments, dispenses herbal medicine, and conducts rituals and ceremonies to ensure the wellbeing of her people. As both a healer and a guide, her wisdom and innate capacity to decipher the divine messages offer a holistic, integrative approach to healing and well-being.

The spectrum of ancient African spirituality witnessed women as the crux of an intricate web of beliefs, rituals, and practices that encompassed the entire spectrum of human experience. From the depths of the sacred Nile in Nubia to the fertile valleys of the Yoruba heartland, the resilient spirit of the feminine divine resonated in the subtle reverberations of the cosmos. In their roles as priestesses, women invoked not just the nurturing, life-giving aspect of the divine but also the transformative, regenerative potential that lies at the heart of all spiritual traditions. Their impact transcended their roles as guardians of the sacred, as their influences resonated deeply within the realms of social, political, and cultural life.

Let us now cast a forward gaze upon the African continent, allowing the wisdom of our ancestral priestesses to percolate into the present, infusing the spiritual traditions of the African diaspora with the underlying essence of our ancient past. These powerful priestesses serve as an indelible reminder of the ongoing communion we hold with our ancestors and the endless reservoir of spiritual strength and resilience that lies at the heart of our collective identity. The knowledge that our ancestors once triumphed over adversity, guided by sagacious women as they negotiated the labyrinthine pathways of the mortal and the metaphysical anchors us in a deeper understanding of our potential and our purpose on this earth.

Shieldmaidens and Strategists: Warrior Women Shaping Africa

As the world turned its gaze to the northeastern reaches of Africa, the Kingdom of Kush, nestled along the Nile River, witnessed the rise of a fearsome warrior queen, Amanirenas. Emboldened by her resolve to repel Roman encroachment into Nubian territory, Amanirenas mustered her forces into a formidable war machine, defying the axis of imperial hegemony. Her relentless campaigns against the Romans led to several successful engagements, dazzling the world with the prowess of a queen unyielding in the defense of her domain. Amanirenas' military genius enabled her to wear down Roman invaders and negotiate a favorable treaty that protected her kingdom's territorial integrity.

Journeying westward to the Hausa city-states of modern-day Nigeria, we stumble upon the charismatic Queen Amina, who defied convention through her insistence on combat training and thus earned her position among the elite ranks of her society's warriors. A skilled equestrian and master tactician, Amina wielded her military expertise to orchestrate a series of conquests, ultimately expanding the boundaries of her kingdom and solidifying its supremacy over rival city-states. Queen Amina's exploits and military conquests altered the geopolitical landscape in her favor, inspiring future generations of African women.

Beyond the scintillating sands of the Sahara, the winds whisper the spectral story of the Aït Ba Amrane warrior-poetess, Lalla Fadhma n Soumer. Armed with the versatile weapons of her quill and sword, Lalla Fadhma led an extraordinary resistance against French colonization in 19th-century Algeria. Heavily influenced by her spiritual beliefs, she merged her zeal with her martial acumen to organize her people and engage in guerilla warfare against the invading Europeans. The shockwaves of Lalla Fadhma's revolutionary fervor reverberated through the hills of Kabylia, awakening a prideful flame amidst the chaos of her people's tribulation.

Throughout this expedition into the heart of ancient Africa, we encounter various artistic and literary allusions to the existence and accomplishments of female warriors. The African oral tradition relays the stirring narrative of the Gudit, the legendary Ethiopian queen who wreaked havoc upon the Kingdoms of Aksum and Zagwe. The Ferraz, the all-female elite corps of Susu Muslim chief Samori Touré, galvanized the cavalries of Guinea as they rode fearlessly into the maw of battle. The Luba Empire of present-day Democratic Republic of Congo bore witness to the ferocity of female warriors, who fought alongside their male counterparts to protect and defend their civilization.

As we marvel at the courage, tenacity, and gallantry displayed by these ancient African warrior-queens and strategists, we begin to discern a deeper truth about the potential for female empowerment and leadership in times of conflict and distress. Equipped with both martial skill and strategic prowess, these remarkable women forged their own destinies rather than meekly submitting to the dictates of others. Their stories served to nourish the spirit of African womanhood, infusing it with an indomitable essence of resilience and determination that would lay the groundwork for future generations of Black women to unleash their innate potential for greatness.

With the tides of time inexorably ebbing and flowing, we can still glimpse the reflections of these tenacious women in the stories of modern-day heroes who dedicate their lives to the pursuit of justice, equality, and empowerment. The vibrant hues of our warrior-queen ancestors continue to shine through the generations that followed in their stead, creating a tapestry of empowered resilience - a living, breathing legacy that allows us to emerge from the challenges of the present as architects of a more equitable and harmonious future.

Legends of Yesteryear: Celebrating Nefertiti, Amina, and Asantewaa

As we traverse the waning sands of time, a troika of illustrious ancient African matriarchs emerge, beckoning us to contemplate their enchanting legacy. Though separated by both time and space, these indomitable women – Queen Nefertiti, Queen Amina, and Yaa Asantewaa – were all catalysts in challenging prevailing norms and nurturing the seeds of power to flourish in the soil of their respective civilizations.

The illustrious figure of Queen Nefertiti materializes from the nether shadows of antiquity, enchanting us with her supernal beauty and enigmatic charm. As the Great Royal Wife of Pharaoh Akhenaton, Nefertiti played a critical role in elevating the status of the Aten deity, a monotheistic, solar-centric vision that disrupted the traditional pantheist worship of ancient Egypt. During her reign, she bore not only the spiritual mantle of the divine, but also participated actively in the daily affairs of her people, an unprecedented feat for a queen. Nefertiti's influence was especially felt within the realm of the arts, as she presided over the Amarna period, a time defined by a unique aesthetic characterized by a naturalistic, radiant visual style. Through her spirited resilience and vision, Queen Nefertiti illuminated the Egyptian consciousness with a novel cosmogony that resonated beyond the confines of her era.

As we journey farther along the ancestral African tapestry, we arrive at the golden gates of the Hausa city-state of Zazzau in present-day Nigeria. Here, we find the influential Queen Amina, a multifaceted warrior who ruled in the late 16th century. Amina's unquenchable thirst for martial prowess and intellectual acuity propelled her to unprecedented heights within her society, as she honed her strategic expertise and deftly navigated the labyrinthine geo-politics of her time. Employing her military acumen and indomitable spirit, Amina's legendary reign is marked by a seemingly insatiable expansionist zeal, as she conquered neighboring city-states and solidified Zazzau's status as an unrivaled regional power. In the annals of African history, Queen Amina's indelible mark on the Hausa civilization reminds us of the latent potential of our ancient, ascendant matriarchs.

Finally, we arrive at the cusp of the 20th century, yet our journey is far from complete. As we delve into the embrace of the resurgent Ashanti Empire in present-day Ghana, we encounter the indomitable presence of Yaa Asantewaa, the warrior queen who fiercely defied the might of the British Empire. Laying claim to her rightful heritage as a queen mother, Yaa Asantewaa led the Ashanti people in their legendary uprising against colonial oppression during the War of the Golden Stool. Though far from the paradigms of conventional warfare, Yaa Asantewaa nonetheless marshaled her forces with a strategic verve that belied her lack of traditional military experience. Fueled by her conviction that the Ashanti people could not be subjugated, Yaa Asantewaa orchestrated an extraordinary resistance against their colonial subjugators, wielding a fearless determination that would come to define the legacy of her reign. Though ultimately defeated, the memory of her courageous stand lives on as an enduring symbol of the unconquerable spirit of Africa's indefatigable matriarchs.

These legendary women – Queen Nefertiti of Egypt, Queen Amina of Zazzau, and Yaa Asantewaa of the Ashanti Empire – share more than just the mantle of regal femininity. Their captivating tales of power, determination, and vision bespeak a collective legacy of strength and resilience that continues to reverberate throughout the generations. As we cast our gaze upon these luminous figures, we glean a vital and profound truth about the indelible influence of women as agents of change in the annals of African history.

In the shimmering mosaic of our enlightened past, these ancient matriarchs serve not only as beacons of feminine power and determination but also as touchstones of inspiration for their myriad descendants. As we stand on the precipice of our own spiritual and historical odyssey, we may choose to summon their legacy – to invoke the hallowed spirits of Queen Nefertiti, Queen Amina, and Yaa

Asantewaa – as befits the diverse, resplendent tapestry of our African heritage.

As we pause at the crossroads of our epochal journey, we may come to recognize the otherworldly configurations that align our ancestral constellations. From the primordial, solarized wisdom of Nefertiti to the martial ardor of Amina, and finally, to the earthbound strength of Yaa Asantewaa, our saga of empowered female leadership transcends the confines of temporal and spatial disparities. It is through the kaleidoscopic legacy of these exemplary women that we can glean the irrepressible impetus of our own potential, as we continue to rewrite the ancestral script of our own resplendent destiny.

Echoes of the Ancestors: How Ancient Matriarchs Mold Us Today

Embarking on a myriad journey through the annals of African history, we encounter an array of fascinating matriarchs—time-tested symbols of power, influence, and resilience. To understand their impact and legacy today, we must delve into the intricate interplay between history, memory, and the African Diaspora.

The echoes of these ancient matriarchs reverberate across the African Diaspora, their stories immortalized through art, oral traditions, and cultural forms. These timeless tales travel on the wings of memory, transcending temporal constraints and imbuing the lives of Black women today with the essence of their intrepid forebearers. As repositories of an indomitable spirit and carriers of ancestral wisdom, these matriarchs shaped the cultural milieu of myriad communities throughout the Americas and beyond, forging a unilinear connection between past and present.

From the vibrant rhythms of the Caribbean to the infectious energy of the African-American South, we can discern the traces of ancient matriarchs in the unique customs, rituals, and expressions of their descendants. Rooted in the rich tapestry of African heritage and infused with a distinct New World sensibility, these traditions exemplify the adaptive nature of Black women across space and time. This ever-evolving cultural synthesis speaks to the profound influence of the ancient African matriarchs, whose indomitable spirits continue to guide and inspire.

In the visual arts, we encounter the shades of these matriarchs in the works of contemporary painters and sculptors, who celebrate and elevate the myriad expressions of Black femininity. Anointing canvas and clay with the ancestral essence of Nefertiti, Amina, and Yaa Asantewaa, these creatives reveal a nuanced visual lexicon, invoking the resilience, wisdom, and power of their forbearers. Through their work, these artists challenge prevailing Eurocentric notions of beauty while simultaneously asserting the validity and viability of an Afrocentric aesthetic.

Similarly, the importance of oral tradition exists as a vital conduit for preserving the legacies of ancient African matriarchs. Stories passed down through generations keep their memories alive, imprinting the hearts and minds of listeners. These tales not only imbue the existence of these women with a sense of immortality but also foment a fervent pride in the rich cultural traditions of the African Diaspora. As the verses traverse through generations, the legacy of these matriarchs is continually reaffirmed and revitalized.

In the realm of education, the lessons conveyed by ancient African matriarchs offer palpable examples of the limitless potential and boundless achievements possible for Black women. By integrating the stories of these remarkable women into curricula, teachers can foster a sense of pride, unity, and empowerment among young students of African descent. Uncovering their stories excavates an empowering lineage that both affirms and fortifies the innate capabilities of Black girls and women.

The legacy of these ancient matriarchs manifests in the spiritual experiences of many Black women throughout the Diaspora. Tapping into a deep well of ancestral wisdom, contemporary women can draw strength and resilience from the example set by these trailblazing spiritual leaders. The sheer tenacity and determination exhibited by these women in the face of adversity serve as an enduring testament to the power of faith and the indomitable nature of the human spirit.

As we stand at the precipice of a new epoch in the ongoing story of the African Diaspora, it is crucial that we continue to honor and cherish the profound impact of the ancient matriarchs. Their stories serve as both a testament to a powerful legacy and a call to action for future generations. In recognizing the indomitable spirit and indelible wisdom embodied by these timeless figures, we can empower Black women to rise above their circumstances, harnessing the rich potential of their ancestral roots to forge a brighter, more equitable future.

Thus, the legacy of ancient African matriarchs can be embraced as an affirmation of our collective resilience, a celebration of our rich heritage, and the foundation for a new narrative—one that foregrounds the strength, beauty, and brilliance of Black women as architects of a transfigured future. As we continue to honor their stories, we simultaneously bring forth the latent potential for greatness inhabiting the hearts and minds of those who follow in their footsteps.

Roots Reclaimed: The Inspirational Legacy of Our Foremothers

Harkening back to the archaic annals of time, we are enshrouded in the mysteries and wisdom of our foremothers; our collective female African ancestry sequestered in the marrow of our very bones. A silent symphony, their indelible presence whispers of an ancient legacy, imbuing the Black woman with an intuitive understanding of her innate resilience and strength. To rediscover our roots, to delve into the syncretic continuum of time to grasp the threads that bind the past, present, and future generations of Black women is a pilgrimage of reverence, discovery, and inspiration.

Gazing into the reflecting pool of centuries gone by, we unearth stories of survival, ingenuity, and power. From the delicate brushstrokes of a once-lost painting depicting the regal Nefertiti, to the commanding visage of Yaa Asantewaa etched in the contours of a bronze statue, these symbols are testaments to the lasting imprint made by our matriarchal ancestors. In juxtaposition to the struggles and strife faced by contemporary Black women, these powerful icons act as beacons of fortitude, instilling within them a steely resolve to conquer adversity and forge their unique path through history.

Indeed, the veneration of the ancient matriarchs serves to connect Black women across generations, reaffirming a shared lineage and instilling a sense of solidarity that surmounts temporal and spatial confines. In the act of researching, retelling, and reclaiming the hidden gems of our ancestral narrative, burgeoning contemporary Black women awaken to the full spectrum of their potential, breaking free from socio-cultural constraints that have so often sought to subjugate and disenfranchise their voices.

This connection with the past disrupts hegemonic narratives, propelling Black women into a blooming space of self-actualization and realization of their boundless capabilities. Inspired by the pugnacity and ingenuity of the ancient matriarchs, they wield the double-edged sword of wisdom and experience handed down through generations, to challenge prevailing norms, question dominant ideologies, and disrupt oppressive systems that have long sought to mute their voices.

Turning the gaze inwards, the evocation of these primordial roots propels a psychological revolution, a transmutation of the self-perception of the Black woman; the litany of her previous traumas, exclusion, and invisibility crystallizing into a powerful armor adorned with the badges of honor and victories bestowed upon her by the matriarchs. In this swelling tide of awareness and spiritual transformation, a new identity dawns, characterized by an unwavering determination to transcend every barrier that would seek to confine her potential.

These newfound insights do not merely linger in the private recesses of the individual psyche: they catalyze a collective momentum. Like an unstoppable river coursing through the ravines of time, this epiphany of self-coalesces into a steady stream of cascading conversations, fostering intergenerational bonding and igniting a sense of purpose among Black women in the pursuit of a shared vision of empowerment and emancipation. Such synergistic alchemy serves to enrich sociocultural, political, and artistic landscapes, potentiating the rise of luminous female voices in every sphere.

As the echoes of the ancestral matriarchs reverberate through the hearts and minds of contemporary Black women, the journey of rediscovering these roots is an integral part of crafting a new legacy that recognizes the resilience, strength, and indomitable spirit of the indigo children of the Diaspora. Fueled by the fire of ancient wisdom and the cosmic imprints of a fabled lineage, they embark on a sacred quest to chart their remaining odyssey, unfurling the star-studded tapestry of a destiny that transcends pre-defined limitations and is illuminated by the shimmering beacons of glorious victories yet to be won.

SOULFUL HERITAGE: EXPLORING THE SPIRITUAL DEPTH OF BLACK WOMANHOOD

In the very marrow of their bones, Black women bear the indelible essence of the spiritual traditions and beliefs bequeathed by their ancestral forebears. Spanning across millennia and the vast expanses of the African continent, these traditions have long formed the bedrock of the Black female experience, interlacing the disparate threads of their collective existence into a rich tapestry of memory, resilience, and self-realization. As they traverse the labyrinth of time, these beliefs become catalysts for spiritual awakening, unfolding layers of storied wisdom and ancestral knowledge that resonate in the pulsating beat of the Black woman's heart.

The genesis of this spiritual wealth can be traced back to the primordial landscape of the African motherland, where the sacred and the profane coalesce in eternal harmony. In this elemental crucible, myriad spiritual traditions emerged, reflecting the kaleidoscopic diversity of the continent's cultures and peoples. Yet beneath the surface of their distinct expressions, there exists a unifying commonality: the veneration of the divine feminine principle as a vital source of life, strength, and wisdom—an enduring testament to the power and resilience of Black womanhood.

These ancient spiritual traditions penetrate the labyrinthine recesses of history, continuing to wield a profound influence on the spiritual lives and practices of Black women across the African Diaspora. From the shores of the Caribbean to the bustling urban centers of the Americas, the echoes of ancestral beliefs and rituals whisper and cajole, resounding with the captivating cadences of the drum, the mystifying incantations of the priestess, and the hypnotic sway of the dancer. They permeate the quotidian fabric of their lived reality, metamorphosing and adapting to the unique cultural milieus and socio-political dynamics encountered on their migratory sojourn, yet retaining their essential essence and capacity for nourishing the soul.

As spiritual lifelines tethered to their ancestral roots, these diverse beliefs and traditions enable Black women to confront and surmount the manifold adversities and challenges that have assailed them throughout the course of history. They draw inspiration and sustenance from the pantheon of divine and ancestral entities revered in their spiritual practices—such as the venerable Yoruba goddess Yemaya, the nurturing maternal spirit of the Niger River, and the fierce Haitian Vodou warrior woman, Ezili Dantor—who embody and exemplify the indomitable spirit and boundless determination inherent in the collective consciousness of Black womanhood.

At a more intimate level, spiritual beliefs and rituals serve as conduits for forging a resilient sense of self and purpose, allowing Black women to navigate the ever-shifting currents of their personal and collective experiences with equanimity and insight. Through prayer, meditation, dreams, and creative expression, they tap into the wellspring of ancestral wisdom and receive guidance, solace, and empowerment. For many, this deep communion with their spiritual heritage imbues their existence with a sense of sacredness and meaning, instilling within them the conviction that they are part of a larger cosmic order, interconnected with the sweep of time and the expanse of the universe.

Furthermore, spiritual practices and beliefs often serve as cornerstones for fostering community, unity, and collective empowerment. In the gatherings of the sacred and profane, Black women congregate to support one another, bearing witness to their shared experiences of struggle, triumph, and transcendence. They weave together the narratives of their individual and collective journeys, fostering intergenerational bonds of solidarity and wisdom that nourish the soul and fortify the spirit against the tide of adversity. Coaxing forth the ancestral voices that reverberate in the marrow of their bones, they reinforce their unbroken lineage of strength and resilience, ensuring that this profound spiritual legacy continues to animate and inspire future generations of Black women.

In this mystical interplay of sacred traditions and lived experiences, an enchanted nexus materializes: a space where the raw intensity of the African drumbeat echoes through the ages, stirring ancestral souls to commune with their descendants as kindred spirits, revealing a world where the resilient roots of Black womanhood form an eternal flowering of the soul. As Black women embrace this timeless spiritual heritage, they lay the foundation for an indomitable self-realization, transcending the entrenched socio-cultural barriers that have long sought to fetter and silence their voices. In so doing, they pay homage to the primal wellspring from which they emerged, and chart a transformative path towards emancipation and empowerment that is as boundless as the cosmos, as perpetual as the human spirit, and as abiding as the hive-mind of the hive-minded: the soul of Black womanhood.

Ancestral Echoes: Unearthing Our Spiritual Foundations

In the genesis of human history, the primordial landscape of Africa bore witness to the birth of a spiritual heritage that would permeate the very essence of the Black woman's experience. A rich and diverse tapestry of spiritual beliefs and practices wove its way through the lives of African women, imbuing their existence with sacred meaning and anchoring their souls to the wisdom and guidance of a timeless ancestral lineage. Though the specific traditions and expressions of spirituality varied across the continent's many cultures, a common thread emerged: the veneration of the divine feminine as a vital source of life, power, and wisdom—a testament to the primordial essence of Black womanhood.

The roots of this spiritual wealth can be traced back to the ancient cultures of Saharan and Sub-Saharan Africa. From the deserts of Egypt to the fertile crescents of the Nile, indigenous spiritual systems flourished and evolved, resonating with the ebb and flow of cosmic cycles and natural phenomena. The divine was seen as manifesting in the natural world, the celestial sphere, and the material plane, an omnipresent force that entwined itself with the lives and destinies of the people. Among these manifold expressions, the veneration of the divine feminine was particularly prominent, exemplified in various goddesses and ancestral entities revered within these ancient societies.

For instance, consider the figure of Isis, the Great Mother in ancient Egyptian worship. Isis was considered the embodiment of fertility, magic, and the afterlife, and her cult resonated across the sands of the ancient African landscape. She symbolized the sources of life-giving elements and was the archetypal divine mother worshipped by women from all walks of life. Through identification with Isis, women could harness an intuitive understanding of the cycles and patterns of life, wield their innate capacities for healing and nurture, and draw upon the inexhaustible reservoir of inner strength forged through the toil of motherhood.

Further within the heart of Africa, numerous indigenous spiritual systems emerged, highlighting the interconnectedness of humankind with the natural world and the cosmos. In these traditions, reverence for the divine feminine was ubiquitous, personified in a myriad of entities that represented aspects of femininity and womanhood. In the Yoruba religion, for example, Yemaya, the goddess of the ocean, held dominion over all waters, including the seas of human emotion. Symbolized by a large, pregnant figure, Yemaya embodies the role of the divine mother, nurturing and nourishing all living beings.

These ancient spiritual traditions, indigenous to Africa, have profoundly impacted the spirituality of Black women, even as the ancestors migrated across continents over the course of millennia. Exiled from their motherland to the far-flung reaches of the New World, enslaved African women endured unspeakable hardship and devastation, yet retained an unbreakable connection to their spiritual heritage in the face of adversity. Through the powerful forces of syncretism and adaptation, these ancient spiritual practices were transmuted into new forms and expressions that would indelibly shape the spiritual identities of Black women throughout the African Diaspora.

The trans-Atlantic slave trade and subsequent cultural dislocations uprooted African women from their spiritual roots, threatening to extinguish the eternal flame of their ancestral wisdom. Yet, like the mythical phoenix rising from the ashes, these ancient spiritual traditions evolved and adapted, merging and interweaving with the doctrines and rituals of various indigenous and foreign religions, spawning a vibrant and multifaceted spiritual landscape that continued to sustain the resilience and endurance of Black women and their descendants.

The diverse spiritual traditions of the African Diaspora encompass a wide array of beliefs and practices that originated from varied corners of the African continent, and, as such, have naturally assumed unique expressions and identities within different geographical and cultural contexts. However, what remains unalterable in these spiritual practices is the intrinsic connection with the ancestral source, the pulsating heartbeat of the motherland that echoes through the ages, reminding Black women of their inherent power, resilience, and wisdom.

Ancient spiritual practices have thus served as the lifeblood and custodians of Black women's identity and experience, offering a vital link to the past and a potent source of resilience in the face of the manifold challenges and oppressions that have sought to silence and subjugate them. Through their diverse manifestations and adaptations across time and space, these spiritual traditions have forged a resilient spiritual bond that unites Black women in the collective embrace of a shared heritage—a spiritual legacy that transcends the ravages of time and the vagaries of history, birthing a transcendent sisterhood that speaks across generations, continents, and the chasms of the human heart.

Spiritual Melting Pot: The Diaspora's Tapestry of Faiths

As the variegated strands of the African Diaspora extended across the teeming shores of the New World, the ancestral spiritual traditions that had sustained and nourished the souls of Black women did not merely dissipate into the four winds, but instead, braided together and entwined with diverse indigenous and foreign doctrines, creating new, potent spiritual lifelines that would serve as beacons of resilience and empowerment within their lived reality.

One such example can be found in the birth and evolution of Vodou, a vibrant, syncretic tradition that emerged amidst the crucible of the trans-Atlantic slave trade, from the crucible of the Caribbean island of Haiti. Beneath the shackles of spiritual subjugation and forced conversion to Christianity, the courageous descendants of the Yoruba, Dahomey and Kongo peoples surreptitiously melded the potent symbols and practices of their spiritual heritage with the iconography of the Catholic Saints. This innovative spiritual cocktail not only provided a clandestine refuge for the preservation and expression of their pre-colonial identities but also catalyzed their struggles for liberation and decolonization in the formidable Haitian Revolution.

Through this spiritual osmosis, the indomitable Yoruba goddess Yemaya assumed the sacral mantle of the Madonna of Regla, embodying the multifaceted archetypes of motherly nurture and resilience in both the terrestrial and celestial realms. As a harbinger of not merely the physical but psychological and spiritual sustenance of her devotees, Yemaya became the spiritual figurehead for legions of Black women, nurturing them and providing the spiritual solace and guidance needed in their desperate struggle for survival, liberation and self-realization on a stolen land.

The power of syncretism is also vibrant in the evolution of Candomblé, a complex, syncretic religious tradition that took root in the Northeastern region of Brazil. Forging an intricate and captivating spiritual collage, the enslaved Africans interwove the mystic threads of their Dahomeyan, Yoruba and Bantu spiritual heritage with elements of indigenous Amerindian spirituality and Catholicism. In the mesmerizing twirl of the Candomblé dance, Black women sustained their venerable relationship with their ancestral orishas, communing with their spiritual manifestations through the energizing rhythms of battle drums and the mellifluous warp and weft of ritual chants.

At the very heart of these syncretic spiritual traditions lies the ever-pulsating beat of the African continent: the rich and sacred inheritance of ancestral wisdom, guidance, and power that courses through the veins of the Black woman, connecting her indelibly to the wellspring of her foremothers. In the spiritual meshwork of the African Diaspora, Black women have grafted their own unique mythologies, ritually reconstructing and reconfiguring their relationship with the divine, manifesting an eternal sense of resilience and empowerment in the face of an ever-shifting cultural landscape.

In an unbroken chain of spiritual continuity, these vibrant syncretic traditions have passed through generations, quilting together the diverse threads of history, memory, and the collective unconscious, offering Black women an inexhaustible spiritual reservoir from which to draw strength, inspiration and solace amidst a world fraught with dehumanization, marginalization, and erasure. The resilience and adaptability of these ancient spiritual practices embody the very essence of the Black woman herself – ever-fluid, ever-evolving, and, ultimately, ever-triumphant.

The story of adaptation and syncretism in the spiritual traditions of the African Diaspora is a testament to the unyielding spirit and creative genius of Black women. As the soul navigators of an expansive cosmic terrain, Black women have charted new courses, blazed their own spiritual trails, and celebrated the deep-rooted and unbroken connection between themselves, their ancestors, and the celestial universe. In doing so, they have emerged as the eternal guardians of the spiritual bloodlines that bind together the African motherland and its far-flung descendants, forging an indelible lineage of resilience and empowerment that will resonate through the ages, undiminished by the vicissitudes of time.

Empowerment Through Faith: The Spiritual Strength of Black Women

Throughout the annals of history, spirituality has served as a profound source of resistance and empowerment for Black women in a world that has often sought to dehumanize and subjugate them. Across the diaspora, the sacred wisdom and knowledge bequeathed by their African ancestors have endowed generations of Black women with the spiritual fortitude and resilience to not only survive—but thrive—in the face of formidable injustice and adversity. By invoking the divine feminine and harnessing the innate spiritual power that flows through their very veins, Black women have emerged as formidable champions of freedom, justice, and healing, wielding the sacred mantle of their spirituality as both a shield and a beacon of hope.

At the heart of Black women's spiritual resistance lies the indomitable spirit of the warrior ancestress—a dauntless force that embodies their unwavering commitment to justice, truth, and liberation. The Yoruba goddess Oya—goddess of storms, transformation, and ancestral connections—epitomizes this elemental force, her fierce and tempestuous energy serving as a spiritual reservoir from which Black women can draw strength, courage, and power in their struggles for emancipation and equality. Through rites, rituals, and sacred storytelling, Black women have forged an unbreakable kinship with these warrior ancestors, channeling their valiant spirits and divine wisdom to dismantle the oppressive forces that have sought to cage their very souls.

In the crucible of the American Civil Rights Movement, spirituality emerged as a potent source of solace, inspiration, and mobilization for countless Black women, many of whom played critical but often underrecognized roles in the struggle for racial equality. The example of Fannie Lou Hamer, a sharecropper turned civil rights activist, illuminates the transformative power of spirituality in fuelling Black women's resistance. Grounded in her deep faith and guided by her indomitable spirit, Hamer became a galvanizing force in the fight for voting rights, her mobilization efforts culminating in her landmark speech at the 1964 Democratic National Convention, where she famously declared, "I'm sick and tired of being sick and tired." In moments of exhaustion and despair, it was Hamer's spirituality—a wellspring of solace and purpose—that fortified her resolve and imbued her with the strength to fight on.

In tandem with their ancestors' guidance, Black women have also wielded their spirituality as a powerful instrument of healing and transformation within the collective strife of their communities. In the wake of trauma and tragedy, Black women have gathered together in sacred spaces—whether in churches, homes, or community centers— to meld their souls, bear witness to one another's pain, and invoke the spiritual energies of hope, compassion, and renewal. Through shared prayers, rituals, and acts of commemoration, they have cultivated a vibrant, spiritually-enriched sisterhood that transcends the boundaries of space and time, fostering deep connections to the ancestral past and a collective fortitude to confront the challenges of the present and future.

The Black Feminist Movement further underscores the integral role of spiritual resistance and empowerment in Black women's struggle for liberation. Bell Hooks, a distinguished scholar and activist, posits that "[Spirituality] is essential for our struggle to self-actualize because it enables us to become warriors in our own hearts, actively fighting against the darkness of self-hatred, despair, and internalized oppression." Embracing this spiritual warrior ethos, Black women have sought to dismantle the pernicious narratives of racial and gender inferiority, cultivating an inner sanctuary of self-love, acceptance, and liberation, which, in turn, enables them to confront external systems of oppression.

Thus, spirituality has been and continues to be an immeasurable source of resistance and empowerment for Black women, its influence profoundly shaping their lives and destinies. It is through this sacred bond with the ancestral past and the cosmic divine that Black women have been able to rise above the myriad of challenges they have faced and continue to face in a world that often fails to recognize their humanity. As the spiritual flame passed down through countless generations continues to burn within the hearts of Black women everywhere, it serves as a poignant reminder of the brilliant, resilient lineage of which they are a part. Empowered by spiritual resilience, Black women will sculpt the landscape of progress, lifting their voices like Oya's tempest, and create a newfound harmony that permeates the chords of both the human heart and the celestial spheres.

Healing Hands: The Restorative Power of Spiritual Practices

As we traverse the complex and multifaceted tapestry of Black women's spirituality, one central theme emerges as a unifying force: the innate capacity for spiritual practices to heal the wounds inflicted by a world that has often sought to marginalize, dehumanize, and subjugate them. It is through these healing rituals – the stitches that mend the tattered fabric of the soul – that Black women have found solace and renewal, fortifying their resilience and empowering their ongoing struggles for liberation and self-realization.

The power of Black women's spiritual practices to provide healing and nurturance to the soul resides in their intimate connection to both the ancestral realm and the sacred cosmos. In invoking the wisdom and guidance of the ancestral matriarchs who came before them, Black women draw upon streams of knowledge and experience that course through the annals of time, providing them with an inexhaustible reservoir of spiritual strength, sustenance, and fortitude. At the same time, they embrace the cosmic energies of the universe, the elemental forces that underpin the very fabric of creation, and channel them into their spiritual practices in pursuit of balance, harmony, and wholeness.

One such spiritual practice exemplifying this transformative process of healing and nurturance is the pouring of libations – a ritual act of offering to the ancestors, the living and the divine. Through the act of pouring sacred water, oil, or other substances onto the ground, an altar, or into a ritual vessel, Black women call forth the spirits of their ancestors and actively engage in dialogue with the multitudes who have come before them. By acknowledging the sacrifices, triumphs, and wisdom of their ancestral progenitors, Black women re-establish a vital connection to a sacred heritage that has often been forcibly severed by the traumas of captivity, colonization, and displacement.

Another powerful mode of spiritual healing prevalent across the African Diaspora is the practice of spiritual baths – ritual cleansings with water infused with herbs, flowers, and sacred objects that purify the body, spirit, and soul. Whether performed in the tranquil sanctum of their homes or as part of elaborate ceremonies within spiritual communities, these baths represent a potent medium for cleansing accumulated spiritual debris, dispelling negative energies, and restoring balance to the physical, emotional, and spiritual planes. For Black women, who have often borne the brunt of intergenerational trauma and sociocultural adversity, spiritual baths serve as a revitalizing source of renewal, self-care, and empowerment.

The profound healing power of communal rituals, too, cannot be underestimated. In the sacred spaces of their spiritual communities, Black women forge invaluable bonds of sisterhood, bearing witness to one another's pain, sorrow, and triumphs, and collectively embarking upon the path of healing and transformation. Through shared prayers, collective song and dance, and the exchange of wisdom and counsel, they create a sanctuary of hope, love, and unity that transcends the mundane confines of their lived reality, offering an invaluable refuge for their weary souls.

Moreover, the rich tapestry of sacred healing practices adopted by Black women extends far beyond the boundaries of religious tradition. Throughout the labyrinthine galleries of their artistic expression – in the vibrant pigments of their paintbrushes, the mellifluous cadences of their poetry, and the supple fluidity of their choreography – they reclaim their agency, rediscover their authentic voices, and weave new allegories of healing, resilience, and empowerment, stitching together the fragments of their shattered selves and reconstituting a tapestry of resilience that is wholly their own.

As we stand at the crossroads of history and memory, bearing witness to the ever-evolving spiritual odyssey of Black women, we must acknowledge the profound role that healing and community play in the sustenance and nurturance of their souls. It is within the sacred crucibles of their spiritual practices – the hallowed spaces where ancient wisdom intermingles with the immutable energies of the cosmos – that Black women gather the golden threads of resilience, weaving them into an unbreakable tapestry that will shelter and uplift them as they stride toward the dawn of a new era. An era in which the sacred mantle of their ancestral legacy, encased in a resilient spirit, will illuminate the path of liberation, illuminating the iyanla, the cosmic road of destiny, and enshrine their rightful place on the summit of a world reborn.

Wisdom Across Ages: The Sacred Teachings of Our Elders

Waves of knowledge and wisdom ripple through time, connecting generations of Black women through the nurturing waters of their shared experiences and spiritual beliefs. Like the branches of a mighty tree, the roots of this wisdom stretch far into the ancestral soils, linking the lives of Black women across the ages in a profound, continuous symphony of understanding and growth. It is within this sacred tapestry of intergenerational wisdom that we discover the potent seeds of empowerment, resilience, and enlightenment that have nourished the spirits of Black women, enabling them to overcome the manifold challenges of their journeys and to reclaim their rightful places in the pantheon of human history.

Throughout the African Diaspora, communities have maintained the sacred tradition of honoring the ancestors, invoking their spirits, knowledge, and guidance through rituals, prayers, and storytelling. These acts, both private and communal, have been integral to the preservation and transmission of ancestral wisdom, enabling Black women to tap into the boundless reservoir of knowledge, strength, and spiritual fortitude that flows through their lineage. In so doing, they establish an unbroken chain of spiritual and intellectual inheritance, fostering a vibrant and resilient sisterhood that spans across the generations and becomes an indelible part of their cultural heritage.

As griots, or storytellers, have carried the historical narratives of their people through the annals of time, so too have Black women served as living repositories of wisdom and knowledge, their voices and spirits elevated in their shared spiritual practices and expressions. Within the sacred spaces of their homes, worship, and community gatherings, Black women have forged bonds of kinship, joy, and inspiration with their ancestors, engaging in spirited discourses that echo across the ages, calling up the memories of their matriarchal progenitors while simultaneously weaving the tapestry of their own enduring legacies.

These spiritual dialogues come alive in the oral traditions, the songs and stories that have been sung, whispered, and shouted into the ether since time immemorial. Through these oral exchanges, the voices of Black women's ancestors reverberate with timeless wisdom, their experiences, insights, and beliefs rendered visible and tangible in the lives of their descendants. As Black women engage with these narratives and absorb the wisdom of their lineage, they also add their own voices, experiences, and beliefs to the collective symphony, amplifying and enriching its resonance, ensuring that it will continue to reverberate for generations to come.

One notable example of this intergenerational spiritual transmission is the legacy of the enslaved African women who wove their spiritual beliefs into the threads of their quilts, embedding their sacred symbols and stories within the intricate patterns and designs that adorned these textiles. As they passed on these art forms and knowledge to their daughters and granddaughters, they also bequeathed a powerful spiritual inheritance, one that continues to resonate with the descendants of these women today.

In addition to their sacred rituals and practices, Black women have also harnessed the power of language to bridge the intergenerational gaps between them and their ancestors. By engaging with their elders, learning their language and samplings, and unearthing the stories of their family's past, they break down the barriers of space and time and enter into a profound communion with their forebears, allowing the spirit of their ancestors to infuse their lives and the experiences of their own descendants.

As we bear witness to this potent interplay of wisdom and belief across the generations, we must recognize the vital importance of nurturing and preserving the spiritual threads that bind Black women to their ancestral legacies. By honoring, celebrating, and nurturing these intergenerational connections, we enable Black women to claim their rightful place within the continuum of human history, granting them the capacity to craft a vibrant and powerful narrative that will resound in the hearts and minds of future generations.

As Black women continue to weave the threads of their resilience and spirituality into their lives and the lives of their descendants, we glimpse a remarkable vision of the future – a future in which the wisdom and spiritual traditions of the ancestors are enshrined within a world where sisterhood, unity, and empowerment thrive in abundance. In this world, fortified by the ancestral spirits that illuminate the path through the ages, Black women will continue to rise as warriors, healers, and leaders, igniting a resurgence of hope and enlightenment that will reverberate throughout the spheres of the cosmos, echoing into the vast expanse of time itself.

ARTISTIC REVOLUTION: CLAIMING IDENTITY THROUGH CREATIVITY

The boundless terrain of the arts presents a fecund domain within which Black women have sown the seeds of their spirits, cultivating a garden of indelible expression that serves as a testament to their strength, resilience, and tenacity in the face of adversity. Through a myriad of artistic expressions, Black women have embarked on creative odysseys of self-discovery, reclaiming their identities and asserting their agency by transmuting their experiences, beliefs, and dreams into a resplendent constellation of colors, forms, and symbols that mirror the depths of their souls.

Journeying through the annals of history, we encounter the first stirrings of these spirited sojourns in the ancient rock paintings and cave murals etched by the hands of our African foremothers, their pigments whispering to the dawn of human creativity. As the currents of time wove the threads of historical unfolding, the artistry of Black women continued to evolve, gradually forming an intricate tapestry of expression that would ultimately transcend the boundaries of space and time. Within the artistic spheres of the African Diaspora, these inscriptions of identity and pride continued to flourish, nourishing the cultural and spiritual lifeblood of a people whose legacy had been threatened by the veiled specter of oppression.

The emergence of the Harlem Renaissance, a pivotal epoch in the history of Black artistic expression, signaled the genesis of a renaissance, a creative renewal that would come to encompass the varied dimensions of Black women's existence. As the brushes of such venerated artists as Lois Mailou Jones and Faith Ringgold swept across the canvas in a tempest of color and symbolism, the world beheld the illuminated visage of the Black woman's spirit, radiant and unbroken. In the steady hands of sculptor Edmonia Lewis, the silent corpus of marble and stone was imbued with the breath of life, her figures bearing witness to the complexities and nuances of the Black female experience.

The literary realm, too, provided a fertile landscape within the intricate gardens of Black women's artistic expression, the pens of such visionaries as Nella Larsen and Zora Neale Hurston inscribing the contours of their heroines' lives with vivid strokes of narrative and prose. The poetic voices of Maya Angelou and Audre Lorde transcended the confines of the printed page, their words resonating with the echoes of ancestral wisdom and the immortal chords of the human spirit. Through their powerful literary creations, these Black women authors defied the invisible chains of marginalization and erasure, illuminating the vast expanse of the Black woman's heart.

In the realm of music and dance, Black women have been the embodiment of grace, power, and resilience, their voices and bodies serving as vessels for the expression of their indomitable spirits. As Billie Holiday lent her haunting vocals to the plaintive cry of "Strange Fruit," she bore witness to the enduring injustices inflicted upon her people, while the fiery effervescence of Josephine Baker's dance captivated the world and shattered all preconceived notions of Black female propriety. Black women in the world of music and dance have continually broken barriers and defied expectations, offering a re-invigoration of the artistic landscape with the sheer force of their brilliance and creativity.

Today, a new generation of Black women artists continue the legacy of their artistic foremothers, their innovative expressions redefining the boundaries of identity and representation in new and extraordinary ways. From the mesmerizing visions of filmmaker Ava DuVernay to the incisive observations of writer and essayist Roxane Gay, these trailblazers have woven their creative threads into the ever-evolving tapestry of the Black experience, crafting a vibrant narrative that spans the continuum of time and space.

As we stand at the nexus of the present and the future, we must acknowledge and celebrate the vital role that artistic expression has played in the lives of Black women, both past and present. In the timeless gardens of artistry, they have cultivated a sanctuary, a refuge that has nourished and nurtured the soul, empowering them to reclaim their identities and their voices through the medium of creative expression.

As we continue to bear witness to the blossoming of the Black woman's spirit in the world of the arts, we must also recognize our role as custodians of this sacred inheritance, ensuring that the creative fruits of our mothers and grandmothers continue to nourish future generations, whose artistic voices will resound like a clarion call heralding the dawn of a new era – an era where the enduring tapestry of Black women's artistic expression shall unravel in kaleidoscopic splendor, adorning the firmament of the human spirit with a legacy as luminous and ineffable as the stars themselves.

The Canvas of Our Lives: Arts, Identity, and Empowerment

As the sun's waning rays dance across the horizon, casting its golden light over the sands of time, the seeds of artistic expression begin to take root in the soil of the collective consciousness of Black women. A primordial force pulses through their veins, igniting the creative embers that lay dormant within. From the ancient cave drawings of ancestral African civilizations to the vibrant choruses of contemporary artistic landscapes, the women of the African Diaspora have employed the language of art to inscribe their legacies and shape the tapestry of human history.

The arts have played an indispensable role in preserving and empowering the histories and experiences of Black women, enabling them to give voice to their truths, traverse the gauntlet of marginalization, and claim their rightful place in the constellation of human expression. As guardians of their cultural heritage, Black women have employed the transformative arts as a sanctuary, a bastion in which they channel their resilience and strength to create indelible art endow with hope, inspiration, and a vivid testament to their triumph over adversity.

The path of artistic expression has been laden with obstacles and travails for Black women navigating a world that sought to limit the range of their creative and intellectual aspirations. Yet, undeterred by the imperceptible chains of discrimination and bias, Black women have persisted, forging their narratives through the alchemy of the arts.

From the canvas to the written word, sculpture to music, Black women have woven the legacy of their ancestors and the spirit of their cultural heritage into the fabric of their art, vestiges of which can be observed in the symbolic languages they employ, echoing whispers of ancestral wisdom across the gulfs of time. Such artistic forms have served as catalysts for the creation of unique techniques and expressions, infused with the vibrant textures of Black women's lived experiences.

The historical trajectory of Black women's artistic expression demonstrates a lineage of creativity and resilience that spans across the ages, with each generation refining and expanding upon the artistic vocabularies of their predecessors. As a result, the arts have served as living portals, enabling Black women to traverse the chasms of time and reconnect with their roots as well as with one another, forging bonds of sisterhood, understanding, and empowerment.

In the artistic consortium of the Harlem Renaissance, the likes of painter Lois Mailou Jones and sculptor Augusta Savage challenged the traditionally Eurocentric paradigms that sought to define the contours of artistic discourse, crafting a revived lexicon of Black aesthetic and experience. In the written word, literary luminaries such as Zora Neale Hurston and Gwendolyn Brooks illuminated the sacred coordinates of Black women's lives, inscribing their memories, desires, and dreams into the sacred vaults of artistic posterity.

As Black women navigate the meandering intricacies of their creative paths, they continue to break through the barriers that have sought to encumber their efforts and to shroud their achievements in obscurity. The poignant narratives of Black women artists such as Kara Walker, with her enigmatic silhouettes that explore the legacies of racial violence, and Julie Mehretu, whose kinetic compositions map the cartographies of human history, continue to challenge the boundaries of artistic expression, offering glimpses into the resilient spirit of the Black female experience.

As the legacies of Black women artists reverberate throughout the corridors of time, they continue to provide a powerful testament to the importance of preserving and promoting the histories and identities of the African Diaspora. With each brushstroke, each lyric, each measure of melody, Black women etch their indelible mark upon the annals of human history, their voices resounding across the sempiternal canvas of artistic expression.

The power of art as a vehicle for the preservation and empowerment of Black women's histories remains deeply ingrained within the African Diasporic consciousness, a tangible thread linking the spirits, struggles, and aspirations of generations. For Black women, the sacred spaces created through the arts foster an environment where their narratives can be nurtured, celebrated, and transmitted through the ages.

In conclusion, as we continue to bear witness to the evolving expressions and boundless creativity of Black women, we must remember that the lifelines of art serve not only as vessels of self-expression but also as immortal chronicles of resilience, wisdom, and strength. It is through these creative tapestries that we journey into the heartlands of the Black female experience, encountering the luminous spirits who have lit the way, their beacons guiding our steps forward as we continue to traverse the landscapes of our collective destiny.

Sculpting Resilience: Visual Arts as Tools of Expression

The indomitable legacy of resilience and empowerment has been imprinted on the collective consciousness of Black women through the centuries by the creative outlets of visual arts, such as painting and sculpture. With each stroke of color and swing of the hammer, this vast and vibrant history of the identity of Black women has been intricately carved and painted, transcending the temporal and spatial boundaries to make an unequivocal mark upon the world.

An eternal ode to identity and defiance, the artistic language developed by Black women across time and space whispers to us the stories of our ancestors, reverberates the dreams of our sisters, and maps the intersections of race, gender, and culture in the unfolding tapestry of human history. The burgeoning power of the visual arts— painting and sculpture alike— offers unique expressions and vantage points, capturing and reflecting the essence of a people whose cultural identity and personal fortitude are as profound as the indigo rivers that flow through their veins.

As early as the Harlem Renaissance, Black women painters and sculptors such as Lois Mailou Jones, Augusta Savage, and Selma Burke championed the evolution of an African-American artistic language that challenged the Eurocentric paradigms of beauty, technique, and subject matter. By embracing the principles of African aesthetics, these innovative artists fostered the creation of a distinctly Black visual experience—one characterized by the use of bold colors, patterns, and textures, as well as the depiction of themes that speak to the duality of life in the African Diaspora. One can interpret these artistic hallmarks as a resolute claim to their identity and voice, evoking pride in their African heritage, while simultaneously establishing an unyielding presence amidst adversity and marginalization. Painting and sculpture served not merely as decorative objects, but rather as tangible manifestations of Black women's resilience, tenacity, and agency.

Examining the works of significant Black women artists, one must pause at the likes of Faith Ringgold, whose powerful quilt narratives layer the complexities of the Black female experience with bold, evocative colors and patterns. Through a multifaceted marriage of textiles and paint, Ringgold weaves a vivid counter-narrative that challenges the silencing and erasure of Black women in the chronicles of history. In her seminal work "Tar Beach," she depicts a young Black girl dreaming of the freedom to fly, encompassing a resolute declaration of self-empowerment and imagination in motifs of celestial wanderings and lyrical color.

The oeuvre of artist and sculptor Elizabeth Catlett, too, radiates this passion for identity and resilience in her evocative sculptures of Black female figures. A fusion of grace and resilient beauty, her majestic sculptures break free from the Eurocentric mold of idealized forms. Her powerful bronze and marble creations, like "Negro es Bello" and "Homage to My Black Sisters," resist the limitations imposed upon Black women by a society that seeks to constrain them. In her defiance to such constraints, Catlett transforms cold, inanimate mediums into incandescent declarations of strength and love, a force imbued with an unapologetic embrace of Black womanhood and an assertion of their agency.

This dialogue of resilience continues into the present with prominent contemporary artists such as Kara Walker, whose innovative use of silhouettes stubbornly refuse the confines of a two-dimensional plane, reaching out to ensnare the viewer in a web of unsettling imagery that subverts the romanticized narratives of the Antebellum South. By confronting the viewer with bleak reminders of a painful history, Walker challenges our collective memory and forces us to reexamine our understanding of race, power, and representation. Similarly, Wangechi Mutu's compelling and enigmatic paintings and sculptures explore the complexities of black female identity in a global space, fusing traditional African art forms with contemporary aesthetics to challenge expectations and provoke dialogues that defy imposed labels.

The creative palettes of Black women artists boldly sweep across a vast canvas, revealing a kaleidoscopic array of colors, emotions, and ideas that speak to the depth and breadth of our shared experiences as daughters, mothers, sisters, and ancestors in a world that seeks to bind and temper our spirit. Yet, through the prismatic visions cast by the paintbrush, the hammer, and the chisel, these visionary forces paint axes of liberation that shatter the facade of the ivory tower and carve new pathways for the next generation of aspiring artists, whose tapestries will continue to tell our stories of resilience, triumph, and love.

Words of Power: Literature as a Reflection of the Black Female Soul

The universe of literary expression has proven itself an indispensable instrument in the intricate art of shaping the Black female experience, wielding the transformative power of words to shine a light on the nuanced realms of struggle, heartache, resilience, and joy that form the intricate tapestries of Black women's lives. Through the fluid strokes of prose, poetry, and orature, Black women have etched their voices and stories upon the contours of the collective consciousness, offering generations of readers and listeners an intimate journey into the rich landscapes of a people whose experiences resist the constraints of a single narrative or form.

From the oral traditions of African griots to the searing verses of Maya Angelou, the resonant melodies of Alice Walker's prose to the unapologetic declarations of Ntozake Shange, the voices and words of Black women through the ages have served as visceral vessels, conduits of memory and imagination, emotion and intellect, resistance and transcendence. The written word, in all its guises, has thus become a potent force in the lives of Black women, a medium through which they have navigated the liminal spaces between their authentic selves and the limiting stereotypes assigned to them. By wrestling with the confines of language and form, these storied voices have crafted new pathways through which they have sought to reclaim the silenced and oppressed, and celebrate the strength and resilience of those who have come before and those who will come after.

The literary endeavors of Black women have, inevitably, reflected the tensions and complexities of their lived experiences, as they sought to forge their paths amidst the cacophonous echoes of a society that sought to dictate their narratives and aspirations. Poetry, for instance, has proven a vital artery of Black women's literary expressions, pulsating with the rhythms and cadences of their unique voices, and shaping a space in which they have found solace, liberation, and communion with others. The indelible verses of poets such as Phillis

Wheatley, Gwendolyn Brooks, Audre Lorde, and Nikki Giovanni have transported readers through time and space, awakening in them a shared empathy and resonance that transcends the mundane and the temporal.

The art of prose has also played a transformative role in Black women's literary trajectories, offering a glimpse into the complexities and nuances of their lives, as reflected in the mirror of fiction and nonfiction alike. Legends such as Zora Neale Hurston have braved the tides of marginalization and erasure to illuminate the multifaceted narratives of Black women, capturing the dialects and rhythms of their colloquial speech and painting a vibrant portrait of a community that defies categorization. Amidst the pages of novels and essays, readers encounter the layered experiences and memories of Black women whose struggles and victories are a testament to the boundless power of the human spirit.

Dramaturgy, too, has offered a unique vantage point from which Black women have channeled their visions and experiences into the realm of performance. Ntozake Shange's groundbreaking "choreopoem" For Colored Girls Who Have Considered Suicide/When the Rainbow is Enuf boldly defied the boundaries of conventional theatre, casting her characters in a kaleidoscope of sound, color, and movement that she termed "transformative" and demanding their rightful place in the spectrum of human expression. Through the dynamic interplay of dance, poetry, and song, Shange and her contemporaries have created viscerally charged works that forge a visceral connection between the performers and their audiences, offering a distinctly Black female perspective on the universal struggles of love, loss, redemption, and identity.

Through the alchemy of linguistic expression, these literary pioneers have forged a resplendent tapestry of experiences and ideas that speak to the breadth and depth of the Black female experience. The words and stories they have woven are echoes of the generations who have come before them, as well as beacons of inspiration and hope for those who will follow in their footsteps.

As these voices continue to reverberate across the expanse of time, we must honor the legacies of the Black women whose words have carved a path for us to walk, dancing between the pages of poetry and prose, the spaces between the beats of our collective hearts. As we continue to forge our own narratives, we follow in the footsteps of the literary giants who have shaped our past, and inspire new generations of writers to preserve and craft the stories of our collective destiny. For in the power of words, we find the strength to dismantle the barriers that bind us, to transcend the confines of expectation and stereotype, to redefine and reshape the narratives of our existence, and to carve new visions that celebrate the resilience, courage, wisdom, and love that have persisted across the ages, blossoming like a lotus in the darkest depths of the world's grandest symphony.

Rhythms of Resistance: The Cultural Celebration of Music and Dance

The rhythmic language of music and dance flows through the rich heritage and history of Black women, echoing across time as a fundamental expression of culture, resilience, and joy. As a celebration of the indomitable spirit of Black women, these artistic forms have collectively shaped and strengthened the bonds of sisterhood, inspiring generations to harness their creative power in the face of adversity. Both music and dance span a vibrant spectrum of styles, each infused with the unique cultural influences and narratives that resonate with the hearts and souls of countless Black women.

In the annals of music history, the enduring voices of legendary Black women singers, musicians, and composers have left an indelible imprint on the cultural lexicon of our times. From the deep, sultry tones of Nina Simone to the soaring gospel-infused notes of Mahalia Jackson, these virtuosos have crafted soundscapes that traverse the vast contours of human emotion, capturing the unique struggles and triumphs of their experiences. Moreover, their pioneering the way for new generations of Black women musicians have carved their paths, breaking boundaries within various genres - rock, jazz, blues, soul, R&B, hip-hop, and beyond.

One notable example of a groundbreaking Black woman musician is Sister Rosetta Tharpe, oftentimes regarded as the "Godmother of Rock and Roll." Tharpe's powerful vocals and guitar skills pioneered electric guitar techniques that directly influenced countless rock musicians, transcending the expectations of her time while staying rooted in her gospel music upbringing. Her defiance of conventional boundaries of race, gender, and musical genres went on to inspire the likes of Chuck Berry and Little Richard, ultimately cementing her legacy as an influential figure in the music industry.

Simultaneously, the language of dance has been a vital expression of the Black woman's experience at the intersection of culture, identity, and emotional catharsis. Choreographers and dancers such as Katherine Dunham, Pearl Primus, and Alvin Ailey have developed innovative dance methodologies that blend African, Caribbean, European, and American movements, creating a distinctly Black dance experience. This transformative blend not only celebrates the roots of Black women's cultural heritage but also breaks free from the narrow definitions that sought to constrain them, weaving tales of resilience and beauty in the elegant sweep of arms, the beating of drums, and the pulsating energy of the dance floor.

The indelible legacy of the Nicholas Sisters, for example, represents a stunning example of Black women's impact on the world of dance. As influential tap dancers during the Harlem Renaissance, these sisters, Dorothy and Vivian, presented rhythm tap with fierce innovation, theatricality, and female empowerment. Their fearlessness in breaking racial and gender barriers within a male-dominated dance form speaks to their unyielding pursuit of artistic excellence and recognition.

Together, these artistic languages - music and dance - serve as a testament to the intricate tapestry of the Black woman's experience, as both individual expressions of creativity and collective celebrations of strength, innovation, and resilience. As these songs and dances reverberate through time, they inspire generation after generation to claim their power, harness their talents, and step boldly into uncharted realms of possibility.

Furthermore, the cultural impact of these forms reaches far beyond entertainment, as they have always been potent tools in promoting unity, healing, and resistance during times of social and political struggles. From the drumming circles and dance rituals in the times of slavery as means to preserve African traditions to the civil rights movement, where songs like "We Shall Overcome" became a powerful anthem of resilience and change, Black women have always been inextricably linked with the creation, preservation, and transformation of the musical and dance landscape.

By honoring the legacies of Black women in music and dance, we are not only illuminating the depth and breadth of their contributions to our shared cultural heritage but also empowering younger generations to embrace their roots, redefine the narrative, and step confidently into their futures. In the synchronized rhythm of drums and voices, the assertive plucking of guitar strings, and the elegant whirl of bodies in motion, we find a harmonious celebration of the unique essence of Black womanhood - an echo of identity that dances to the beat of the Black woman's heart, just as her ancestors did, and always will.

Creative Fire: Modern Artists Changing the Narrative

In a world where Black women have been subjected to systemic racism and misogyny, contemporary artists have emerged as powerful voices in the ongoing battle to reclaim and celebrate their identities. Through diverse mediums such as painting, photography, sculpture, and multimedia installations, these visionaries have deftly wielded their artistic prowess to challenge the status quo, shift societal perspectives, and illuminate the multifaceted nature of the Black female experience. The creative expressions of these artists not only reassert the autonomy, individuality, and resilience of Black women but also serve as vibrant beacons of inspiration for generations to come.

Consider the groundbreaking work of Kara Walker, one of the most influential and critically acclaimed contemporary Black women artists of our time. Renowned for her provocative silhouettes that often depict scenes of slavery, violence, and sexuality, Walker's oeuvre delves into the complexities of race, gender, and power in American history. Her monumental installations, such as the 50-foot-tall sugar sphinx she created for her 2014 exhibit A Subtlety, or the Marvelous Sugar Baby, challenge conventional narratives about Black womanhood, urging viewers to confront the intertwined legacies of oppression, exploitation, and resilience that have shaped the lives of countless generations.

Equally transformative is the work of visual artist LaToya Ruby Frazier, whose intimate photographs chronicle the raw, unvarnished experiences of Black women living in impoverished urban landscapes. By capturing the stark realities of life in her hometown of Braddock, Pennsylvania, Frazier's photographs bear witness to the structural inequalities that continue to impact the lives of Black women in postindustrial communities. Her evocative images function as a form of visual activism, sparking much-needed conversations around socioeconomic disparities, environmental racism, and the erasure of Black narratives from mainstream discussions.

In addition to these seminal artistic giants, other contemporary Black women artists have forged new pathways in reimagining and redefining the multitude of stories and identities that comprise the Black female experience. Recently, the art world has been captivated by the meteoric rise of Amy Sherald, who gained worldwide fame for her extraordinary portrait of former First Lady Michelle Obama. Imbued with the artist's signature grayscale palette and infused with a captivating sense of depth and introspection, Sherald's portrayals of Black women transcend traditional portraiture, elevating her subjects to a space of regality, grace, and resilience.

Visual artist Mickalene Thomas, too, has utilized her artistic talents to explore the myriad identities and historical representations of Black women, drawing from art history, popular culture, and fashion. Thomas's glittering, kaleidoscopic collages reflect a striking amalgam of influences - from African textiles to 1970s Blaxploitation films. She boldly challenges the aesthetic conventions of mainstream portrayals, creating dazzling portraiture that celebrates the diversity, beauty, and strength of Black womanhood in all its incarnations.

These artistic endeavors of contemporary Black women artists are laden with the potent force of disruption and reimagination. By daring to push against the limiting and reductive narratives that have long plagued their collective experience, these creatives have forged new trajectories that demand the recognition, respect, and reverence of a long-overlooked community. Their work pays homage to the ancestral legacies that have shaped the lives of Black women, while simultaneously inspiring fresh, innovative explorations of identity, power, and liberation.

As we bear witness to the artistic revolution forged by these contemporary trailblazers, we are reminded of the limitless potential that lies within the hearts, minds, and hands of Black women. Just as they challenge the world to reimagine the possibilities that shimmer within their brushstrokes, their sculptures, and their camera lenses, so too do they encourage other Black women to claim their own narratives, defying the societal constraints that would seek to define them. In the coming years and decades, the influence of these creative visionaries will resonate across generations, ensuring that the true stories and unique perspectives of Black women are no longer relegated to the shadows but are instead triumphantly illuminated by the light of artistic expression. As we stand upon the precipice of this dynamic cultural shift, we can be confident in the knowledge that the indomitable spirit, courage, and resilience of Black women's identities will continue to be vibrantly celebrated by those who follow in the footsteps of these remarkable contemporary artists, paving the way towards a future where all voices are heard, and all stories are seen.

VOICES OF CHANGE: BLACK WOMEN LEADING THE CHARGE IN JUSTICE

Throughout history, the struggle for social justice has always been marked by the presence of indomitable Black women whose voices, actions, and unwavering determination have paved the way for transformative change. These pioneers of the civil rights movement, women's rights, and Black liberation have stepped boldly into the fray, confronting the entrenched systems of inequality and discrimination that have sought to silence their cries for justice. Fearless and unapologetic, these revolutionary visionaries have shaped the course of history, fighting not only for their own rights but also for the rights of generations to come.

One of the earliest and most influential Black women in the fight for social justice was abolitionist and conductor of the Underground Railroad, Harriet Tubman. Born into slavery, Tubman managed to escape and subsequently dedicated her life to liberating others from the chains of bondage. Successful in leading approximately 70 enslaved people to freedom, she became a symbol of hope and defiance in the struggle against slavery. Furthermore, Tubman was a staunch advocate for women's suffrage, working alongside contemporaries such as Susan B. Anthony, to advance the cause of women's political enfranchisement.

Another formidable force in the realm of social justice was Ida B. Wells, a journalist, and activist whose pioneering investigative reporting uncovered the epidemic of lynching in the post-Civil War South. Through her meticulous research and relentless pursuit of the truth, Wells exposed the harrowing scale of this brutal form of racial terror, galvanizing both national and international support for the anti-lynching movement. Beyond her groundbreaking journalism, Wells was also a founding member of the National Association for the Advancement of Colored People (NAACP) and a dedicated advocate for women's suffrage.

The voices of these early trailblazers laid the groundwork for the emergence of critical social justice movements in the twentieth century, including the Civil Rights Movement, which witnessed the rise of several prominent Black women leaders. Women such as Rosa Parks, whose iconic act of civil disobedience galvanized the Montgomery Bus Boycott, and Ella Baker, whose grassroots organizing and community-building efforts were instrumental in the formation of the Student Nonviolent Coordinating Committee (SNCC), demonstrated the power and resilience of Black women in challenging systemic inequality.

For many Black women activists, the fight for racial and gender equality was deeply intertwined. A shining example of this intersectional approach to social justice was embodied in the life and advocacy of Pauli Murray, a lawyer, and activist whose insights into the interconnectedness of racial and gender discrimination led her to develop the legal concept of "intersectionality." Murray's tireless efforts to advance civil rights and women's rights cut across many spheres, including her groundbreaking work on the desegregation of public schools and her co-founding of the National Organization for Women (NOW).

Inspired by the tireless efforts of these pioneering women, future generations also took up the mantle and continued the long march for justice and equality. The Black Panther Party, an organization founded in the late 1960s to combat racial and economic injustice, counted amongst its members a significant number of women who held influential positions and contributed immensely to the Party's programs. Women like Angela Davis, Elaine Brown, and Assata Shakur joined the ranks of the Black Panthers, advocating for systemic change and fearlessly confronting the oppressive forces of racism, sexism, and capitalism.

As the fight for social justice evolved, so too did the prominence of Black feminist thought and activism. Figures such as bell hooks, Audre Lorde, and Kimberlé Crenshaw expanded the discourse on the intersecting struggles faced by Black women, challenging both white-centric feminism and male-dominated civil rights movements to recognize the unique dimensions of oppression experienced at the nexus of race and gender. As the concepts of intersectionality and womanism gained traction, a new generation of revolutionaries arose to confront contemporary manifestations of racial and gender injustice, including police brutality, reproductive rights, and LGBTQ+ rights.

In recent years, contemporary social justice movements echo the storied histories of these revolutionary voices, inspiring a modern generation of Black women activists and leaders. The founding and leadership of the Black Lives Matter movement by Patrisse Cullors, Alicia Garza, and Opal Tometi represent a direct link to the indomitable spirit of their predecessors. The movement's interlocking fight against racial injustice, police brutality, and gender inequality draws upon the wisdom and tenacity of past trailblazers, ensuring that the voices of Black women remain at the forefront of change.

As we reflect on the powerful legacy of these remarkable individuals, we bear witness to the courage and strength that has always been the lifeblood of Black women's pursuit of equity, freedom, and justice. Each of these pioneers has opened doors, broken barriers, and cleared the path for future generations to continue the journey toward a more inclusive and equitable world. In honor of their sacrifices, let us carry forward the torch they have passed, guided by the brilliant light of their wisdom, resilience, and love for humanity. Like a symphony of voices, joining together in a crescendo of hope and determination, their collective impact serves as an enduring testament to the fearless spirit that has, and always will, embody the essence of the Black woman's pursuit of justice.

Marching Through Time: Pioneers in the Fight for Equality

The arduous and grueling journey towards freedom and equality in the United States has been marked by the relentless efforts of countless women of African descent. Their indomitable spirit and unwavering resolve in the face of overwhelming adversity and opposition laid the foundation for the transformative changes that would emanate from their labors. From early abolitionists to key protagonists of the nascent civil rights movement, these women, bound by their tenacious pursuit of justice and equity, forged a legacy of resistance that reverberates through the annals of history.

One cannot delve into the early origins of the fight for freedom without acknowledging the essential contributions of Sojourner Truth. Born into slavery, Truth would go on to claim her liberty in 1826, subsequently dedicating her life to the abolitionist cause. A formidable orator, her famed "Ain't I A Woman?" speech at the 1851 Women's Rights Convention in Akron, Ohio, shone a spotlight on the intersecting oppressions faced by black women, imploring her audience to confront the double burden of racism and sexism. In her tireless activism, which included touring the country as a lecturer and aiding fugitive slaves through her involvement with the Underground Railroad, Sojourner Truth embodied the unrelenting determination that defined the fight for freedom in its early stages.

Parallel to Truth's crusade ran the fierce convictions of Maria Stewart, an oft-overlooked figure in the abolitionist movement. Compelled to act by the insidious bloodshed inflicted upon her race and gender, Stewart emerged as a fiery voice against the enslavement and marginalization of black women—a position that, at the time, placed her at the vanguard of both racial and gender advocacy. Through her groundbreaking lectures and prolific writings, she not only eviscerated the immoral foundations upon which slavery was built but also urged black women to reject their subjugation by seizing education and economic power.

The early fight for freedom also bore witness to the pioneering courage of black women activists who risked their lives to further the cause of emancipatory justice. Harriet Tubman, known widely as the "Moses of her people," epitomized this fearlessness. After a daring escape from slavery, Tubman returned to the South a total of nineteen times to usher approximately 70 individuals to freedom along the arduous journey to the North and to Canada. Despite the perilous nature of her missions, which could have easily led to her permanent recapture or demise, Tubman's unwavering commitment to her people marks her as an inimitable force in the early struggle for liberation.

As a new century dawned, the burgeoning civil rights movement bore witness to a veritable pantheon of black women luminaries who would continue to challenge the status quo and advance the fight for freedom. Foremost among them was Anna Julia Cooper, a prominent intellectual and author whose work centered the unique plight of black women under the weight of racial and gender oppression. Breaking racial and gender barriers in academia, Cooper went on to become the fourth African American woman to earn a Ph.D., further elucidating the boundless potential of black women when armed with education and opportunity.

In examining the relentless fight for freedom spearheaded by early abolitionists and civil rights activists, one cannot help but be awed by the sheer tenacity, courage, and unyielding conviction that characterized their efforts. Combating not only the chains of literal enslavement but also the societal bonds that attempted to keep them in a perpetual state of marginalization and subjugation, these women became essentials forces for change, inspiring generations of abolitionists and rights activists to follow in their footsteps.

As their voices reverberated through time, these early pioneers of freedom imbued the struggle for justice with unyielding determination and unceasing hope. From the impassioned oratory of Sojourner Truth to the steely resolve of Harriet Tubman, they kindled the embers of change that would, over time, ignite a firestorm of transformative social upheaval. Their struggle, their resistance, and their unshakable belief in their inherent worth and dignity echo still in the hearts of those who continue to strive for a more just and equitable world, not only for themselves but for all whose lives have been touched by the long shadow of injustice.

Breaking Barriers: Black Women's Political Journeys

Throughout history, the landscape of political representation for Black women has been traversed by extraordinary individuals whose achievements resonate with defiance, audacity, and a profound sense of duty to the communities they represent. These trailblazers have dismantled barriers of race and gender in their pursuit of impactful leadership, establishing new milestones and expanding the horizons of possibility for generations to come. As we cast our gaze upon these female political figures, we bear witness to the stories of groundbreaking firsts, profound courage, and unwavering conviction, illuminating the agency of Black women in the struggle for progress.

Undoubtedly, one of the most iconic figures in Black women's political leadership was the orator, abolitionist, and black women's rights advocate, Shirley Chisholm. In 1968, Chisholm etched her name into the annals of history as the first Black woman elected to the United States Congress, setting the stage for a transformative tenure in which she championed issues of racial and gender equity, fought against Vietnam War spending, and advocated for the economic empowerment of marginalized communities.

Yet, Chisholm's most groundbreaking moment came in 1972 when she announced her candidacy for the United States presidency, making her the first major-party Black candidate and the first woman ever to seek the Democratic Party's nomination. Though her campaign ultimately proved unsuccessful, the unwavering courage and audacity of her candidacy resonated with the slogan she adopted: "Unbought and Unbossed." Chisholm's political career signified a seismic shift in the potential and possibilities for Black women's participation and influence in the American political sphere.

As Shirley Chisholm's legacy began to reverberate within the chambers of power, new faces emerged, carrying the torch and continuing the fight for representation and equity. Another poignant example of the indefatigable spirit of Black women in politics is Barbara Jordan, a trailblazing attorney and politician who, in 1972, became the first Black woman from a southern state elected to the United States House of Representatives. A skilled orator and fierce advocate for civil rights, Jordan would deliver a keynote address at the 1976 Democratic National Convention that would serve as a clarion call for unity and progress in a troubled America.

Picking up the torch from Chisholm and Jordan, Carol Moseley Braun broke another barrier in the ongoing quest for representation by becoming the first African American woman elected to the United States Senate in 1992. From her passionate advocacy for women's rights to her dedication to ending apartheid in South Africa, Braun's tenure was marked by a unique blend of compassion and unbridled tenacity. In advancing the cause of justice and equality at the highest echelons of political power, Braun imbued a new generation of Black women leaders with a sense of hope and determination.

The political ascent of Black women continued into the 21st century with the election of trailblazers like Ayanna Pressley, the first Black woman to serve on the Boston City Council and the first Black woman to be elected to Congress from Massachusetts; Ilhan Omar, the first Somali-American and one of the first Muslim women to serve in Congress; and, most recently, Kamala Harris, the first Black and South Asian woman elected as the Vice President of the United States. Each of these remarkable women has made history in her own right while simultaneously pushing the boundaries of possibility for future generations of Black leaders.

As these barrier breakers and trailblazers pressed onward and upward, it became increasingly clear that the political power and influence exerted by Black women would not be contained by traditional norms and expectations. From the halls of Congress to the highest office in the land, the fearless spirit of Black women's leadership has consistently shattered glass ceilings and subverted expectations, reshaping the fabric of the American political landscape in the process.

The remarkable accomplishments of these groundbreaking women in political leadership represent the dawning of a new era in which the voices, perspectives, and visions of Black women can no longer be silenced or sidelined. Instead, the legacy of these political pioneers has provided a powerful blueprint for how Black women's leadership can flourish in a complex and often inhospitable terrain. As the torch of their accomplishments is passed from one generation to the next, the indomitable spirit of these women shall forever serve as a lodestar, guiding and inspiring a multitude of others who will rise, impassioned and undeterred, in the quest for justice, equality, and representation in the halls of power. In their ceaseless struggle to dismantle the barriers and shatter the glass ceilings that have long restricted their access to the political arena, these trailblazers have forged a pathway that will, for all time, reverberate with the sound and fury of Black women's footsteps ascending in pursuit of their boundless potential and transformative influence on the world around them.

Fists in the Air: The Firebrands of Black Power and Feminism

The Black Power Movement and Black Feminism were two revolutionary factions that emerged simultaneously in the United States during the 1960s and 1970s, representing both the breadth of radical possibilities and the diversity of Black women's perspectives on freedom and justice. The preceding civil rights movement had provided a foundation of resistance upon which these more militant ideologies could flourish, with Black women playing a crucial role in driving this shift towards a more progressive and empowering vision of societal transformation.

The Black Power Movement, as its name suggests, sought a radical redistribution of political, economic, and social power, vehemently challenging the conventions of white supremacy and systemic racism that had marginalized African Americans for generations. With its roots in the cultural nationalism advocated by Malcolm X and the more militant factions of the civil rights movement, Black Power broke from earlier nonviolent protests and called for African Americans to reclaim their autonomy and dignity through the development of Black political and cultural institutions, as well as through revolutionary acts of self-defense and empowerment.

At the forefront of this movement were women such as Angela Davis, a luminary scholar, and revolutionary who embodied the intersection of race and gender politics with unapologetic radicalism. As an influential leader within the Communist Party USA and the Black Panther Party, Davis' political activism focused on dismantling the many facets of oppression faced by marginalized communities and dismantling the carceral state, which disproportionately targeted African Americans. Her arrest and acquittal on conspiracy charges further galvanized her supporters, making her an indelible symbol of resistance against systemic injustice.

Kathleen Cleaver, another prominent Black Power advocate, similarly advanced the cause through her work within the Black Panther Party, initially serving as the group's national secretary and later evolving into a prolific spokesperson and organizer. Cleaver's passion for racial and gender equity, coupled with her steely resolve in the face of government persecution, made her an iconic figure in the struggle for Black liberation and self-determination.

Running parallel to the Black Power Movement was the emergence of Black Feminism, an ideology that sought to center the voices and perspectives of Black women within both feminist and civil rights discourses. Recognizing that the unique experience of Black women could not be fully encompassed or addressed by either movement independently, Black Feminism emerged as a means of bridging the gap between these seemingly disparate struggles, addressing the intersecting oppressions faced by Black women at the nexus of race, gender, and class.

Pioneering Black feminists such as bell hooks, Audre Lorde, and the Combahee River Collective turned their attention to the disparities between the experiences of white women and women of color, critiquing mainstream feminism's tendency to privilege the former demographic's concerns above those of their more marginalized counterparts. These insightful critiques, paired with a broader emphasis on self-definition and self-empowerment, laid the groundwork for a more inclusive vision of gender justice that would reverberate through both the broader feminist movement and the ongoing struggle for racial equality in the United States.

Ultimately, the radical movements of the Black Power Movement and Black Feminism represented a potent form of resistance by addressing the inextricable links between the myriad fissures of oppression that had long constrained the lives of Black women. By reclaiming their humanity and demanding justice on their own terms, these revolutionaries not only exposed the deeply ingrained biases and prejudices at the heart of American society but also paved the way for future generations of activists to challenge these barriers and envision a more equitable world.

As the echoes of these fierce battles resonate within today's social justice movements, we cannot forget the audacious spirit and unwavering conviction that characterized the work of these radicals and revolutionaries. Through their courageous defiance, these women illuminated a path towards a more just society, forcing a reckoning with the limitations of traditional approaches to civil rights and gender equity. It is their tenacity and insight that would forever change the landscape of activism and resistance, paving the way for a new generation of revolutionaries to continue the fight for justice and representation, beyond the confines of the past and into the uncharted territory of a more inclusive and progressive future.

The New Guard: Today's Movements Shaping Tomorrow

The ascent of contemporary social justice movements heralds a new era in the ongoing struggle for racial equity and justice, with Black women at the forefront of these transformative efforts. As the tides of protest and change swell with renewed urgency, the legacy of past radicals and revolutionaries intertwines with the voices of today's trailblazers, echoing the bold and resolute spirit of generations past.

The Black Lives Matter (BLM) movement is one such emblematic movement, emerging in 2013 in response to the acquittal of Trayvon Martin's murderer. Founded by three Black women – Alicia Garza, Patrisse Cullors, and Opal Tometi – BLM has rapidly gained momentum, penetrating the global consciousness and sparking mass mobilizations against racial injustice worldwide. Rooted in the principles of intersectionality, inclusivity, and a commitment to justice, the BLM movement has become a potent force which energizes and unites millions of people globally to challenge racial biases, police brutality, and systemic racism.

Garza, Cullors, and Tometi's leadership within the BLM movement marries the wisdom of earlier revolutionary voices with the unique challenges of the present day. By centering the experiences and concerns of Black women within the movement, the work of BLM aims to ensure that the legacy of past activists is not forgotten and that the unique struggles faced by Black women are not relegated to the margins of the movement's priorities. At the same time, the founders and subsequent activists within the BLM movement recognize that their vision of justice is a complex endeavor that requires a multifaceted, inclusive approach – one which pulls together disparate threads of activism and resistance into a powerful, unified tapestry.

The BLM movement has inspired numerous offshoots and related movements, each seeking to build upon the energy and momentum generated by the initial spark of resistance. One such movement is the

Say Her Name campaign, spearheaded by the African American Policy Forum and the Center for Intersectionality and Social Policy Studies. This initiative specifically focuses on the often overlooked cases of police brutality against Black women, amplifying their stories and demanding justice for their lost lives. In doing so, the Say Her Name campaign continues the work of Black feminists who have long fought for the inclusion of Black women's voices and experiences within social justice movements.

Another recent and significant movement is the Movement for Black Lives (M4BL), a coalition of organizations and individuals dedicated to fighting for a world in which all Black lives are valued and protected. M4BL champions a wide array of issues, such as criminal justice reform, economic justice, and community empowerment, all while emphasizing the intersectional nature of Black liberation struggles, highlighting the roles and contributions of Black women, LGBTQ+ individuals, and disabled Black people in advancing the cause of racial justice.

In their call to action, contemporary social justice movements such as BLM, Say Her Name, and M4BL evoke the fiery determination of their revolutionary forebears, capturing the spirit of defiance and resilience that characterized the work of Black Power activists and Black feminists in the 1960s and 1970s. However, these movements also break new ground in redefining the parameters of the struggle for racial justice in the 21st century. Through their innovative use of digital technologies, social media platforms, and the power of mass mobilization, these contemporary movements are establishing new arenas for resistance and amplifying their reach far beyond the confines of traditional activist spaces.

As we contemplate the enduring and evolving significance of Black women's leadership within these contemporary social justice movements, we cannot help but marvel at the depth and range of their influence in shaping the course of history. When the torch of resistance is passed from one generation to the next, the indelible imprint of these women's tenacity, courage, and wisdom carries their legacies forward, inspiring countless others to stand up and join the fight for a just, equitable world.

For, as we have seen in the long and storied past of Black women's activism, these pioneers, past and present, have consistently defied expectations, transcending barriers and uniting their communities in the unyielding pursuit of justice. Through their valiant efforts, we stand witness to an ever-burning torch of resistance, its flame steady and resolute, illuminating the uncharted path toward a future in which the promise of racial and gender equity takes a bold, tangible form – a living testament to the indefatigable spirit of Black women everywhere.

UNBREAKABLE BONDS: THE POWER AND IMPORTANCE OF COMMUNITY

The fabric of Black women's histories and experiences is woven from the threads of resilience, perseverance, and triumph over adversity. Their unbreakable bonds of sisterhood and community have provided a foundation upon which to combat the intersecting systems of oppression that have sought to silence and marginalize them for generations. The power of the community lies not only in numbers but in the shared experiences and collective knowledge passed down through generations, the nurturing of relationships, and the promotion of a united front in the face of adversity.

One of the most powerful demonstrations of the importance of community can be found in the historical narrative of enslaved African women who were forcibly brought to the United States. Despite the dehumanizing conditions they faced, Black women created communities of support and resistance amongst themselves that provided a foundation of healing, hope, and collective strength. They sustained their culture and shared memories through storytelling, song, and dance, preserving an identity that could not be taken from them and forming the basis of a strong, defiant community.

In the years since, Black women's communities have continued to develop and adapt to meet the evolving challenges and needs of their members. The benefits of these communities are multifaceted: they provide practical assistance and emotional support, facilitate a shared understanding of their unique experiences, enable the transmission of valuable knowledge and skills, and foster a sense of unity that bolsters the overall drive for change and justice.

Examples of the power of community abound in the lives and legacies of Black women. In the 19th and early 20th centuries, women like Harriet Tubman, Sojourner Truth, and Ida B. Wells harnessed the strength of the communities they had built and nurtured to inspire, lead, and support collective resistance initiatives, like the Underground Railroad, emancipation, and anti-lynching campaigns. Their work provided the foundation for later generations of Black women to build upon as they continued to seek social and political change.

Taking inspiration from these pioneers, Black women across the diaspora have continued to create strong networks based on mutual trust and shared experiences. This solidarity, woven across countries and continents, provides a powerful bulwark against the forces of racism, patriarchy, and systemic injustice. Across the United States, the Caribbean, Africa, and beyond, Black women's community organizations, advocacy groups, and grassroots movements have provided crucial support and resources to those seeking safety, opportunity, and empowerment.

The strength of these communities also lies in their ability to adapt and evolve over time, reflecting the changing needs of their members and the diverse nature of their identity and experiences. Today's Black women navigate an increasingly complex, globalized world, where issues such as climate change, migration, digital connectivity, and culture merge and intersect. As such, their communities must continue to evolve and adapt to meet these new and emerging challenges head-on, while staying grounded in the knowledge, wisdom, and resilience that are integral to the rich tapestry of their shared heritage.

Ultimately, the power and importance of community for Black women lie not only in the tangible resources and support they provide but also in the powerful symbol they represent of resistance, unity, and defiance in the face of adversity. Through these unbreakable bonds, Black women across time have crafted an armor and a strategy: one that sustains and harmonizes the collective voices of the Black women's chorus and responds to the challenge of marginalization with singular and unified determination.

As we look ahead to the unfolding journey of empowerment and social transformation for Black women, the essential role of communities and the bonds they establish remains central. Through these connections, the shared purpose and strength of individuals coalesce into a formidable and transformative force. This force, driven by the shared knowledge, wisdom, strategy, and courage of Black women past and present, ensures that this defiant and resilient spirit will continue to support future generations, buoying them in their pursuit of equity, justice, and the realization of an inclusive, empowering vision of a world where they, too, can truly flourish.

The Role of Community in the Lives of Black Women

The power of community in Black women's lives lies at the very foundation of the enduring strength, tenacity, and resilience that have carried these formidable individuals through generations of adversity. It is within the supportive embrace of a connected community that Black women find solace, validation, and affirmation, as they navigate the tangled web of challenges and barriers woven by intersecting systems of racism, sexism, and discrimination. From the dawn of human civilization to our contemporary globalized world, Black women's communities have provided an essential bedrock of resources, knowledge, and collaboration, which have empowered these extraordinary individuals to confront and dismantle the oppressive forces that have sought to constrain their dreams and aspirations.

An early and indelible testament to the unyielding power of Black women's community lies in the accounts of enslaved African women, who, despite enduring the most dehumanizing conditions known to humankind, found a way to create and sustain communal bonds, resist their oppressors, and nourish their spirits. Far from being mere victims of circumstance, these resilient women forged clandestine communities of mutual support and solace that nurtured their souls and fueled their resolve to never relent in the pursuit of freedom. Through the whispered exchange of stories, songs, and dances infused with the memory of their African heritage, these women repudiated the subjugation that was imposed upon them; asserting their personhood and holding on to cultural roots that could not be erased by the torment of slavery.

In these intimate spaces of sisterhood, defiance was cultivated and the revolutionary spirit was born. One powerful example of this can be found in Maroon communities throughout the Americas — semiautonomous societies of enslaved Africans and their descendants who, through constant resistance and uprising, carved out territories of relative autonomy and self-governance. Primarily composed of

Black women and children, these communities fostered a spirit of resistance and ingenuity that would give rise to new generations of fierce abolitionists, activists, and leaders in the struggles against slavery and oppression.

As the arc of history unfolded and brought with it further waves of adversity and travails, Black women standing on the shoulders of their indomitable ancestors continued to rise and defy any obstacle laid out before them. The 20th century saw the emergence of trailblazing community leaders, such as Madam C.J. Walker, who not only transformed the landscape of Black beauty and entrepreneurial success but also used her influence to create and foster community resources and support systems for Black women to access in pursuit of their own dreams and ambitions.

The powerful influence of community-building continues to reverberate throughout the generations, as evidenced in the diverse and dynamic congregation of Black women across various spheres of society. Be it in the hallowed halls of academia, the cathedrals of artistic expression, or the frontlines of grassroots activism, the enduring, unwavering power of community-building resonates deeply within the tapestry of Black women's lives. It is through this communal framework that today's Black women are empowered to shatter the glass ceilings that still persist and carve out new avenues of innovation, progress, and social transformation.

Inspired by the defiant spirit of their ancestors, contemporary Black women have forged new and innovative strategies for establishing community, harnessing the power of digital technologies, social media, and grassroots activism to create far-reaching networks of support, knowledge sharing, and advocacy. From the Black Lives Matter movement to the Women's March and beyond, Black women's leadership in contemporary community building is testament to the long, unbroken chain of resilience that stretches across the generations, fortifying the dreams and determination of these pioneers with the lessons, wisdom, and hope passed down from the ancestors who walked before them.

The role of community in the lives of Black women cannot be overstated. Reaching back to our African roots, through the turbulent waters of the transatlantic slave trade, and into the present-day fight for racial justice and equality, the power of community remains a thread woven inextricably into the fabric of Black women's existence. By honoring, cultivating, and sustaining the vital bonds that form the lifeblood of our communities, we ensure that the torch of defiant resilience borne by generations of Black women continues to burn bright, illuminating our path forward as we strive to navigate an ever-changing world fraught with fresh challenges and boundless opportunities.

Sisterhood Unbreakable: Circles of Support and Empowerment

Imagine, if you will, a safe space – a loving and nurturing haven where Black women can come together to share their experiences, discuss the challenges they face, and offer support and encouragement to one another. This vision is not just a dream, but a reality that has been shaped by Black women throughout history in the form of sisterhood circles. These groups – both formal and informal – have played a critical role in providing mutual support, education, and empowerment to countless generations of Black women, building the backbone of their communities and charging them with the strength and resolve to take on the world.

Sisterhood circles manifest in various forms and for different purposes – from grassroots organizations and mother-daughter gatherings to book clubs, online forums, and women-led spiritual congregations. Yet, despite their varied nature, the essence remains the same – to nourish the souls and enrich the lives of Black women through the power of connection and camaraderie. In these circles, the women find comfort in knowing that their sisters understand the unique intersections of race and gender they face daily. They are united by the recognition of their shared experiences as well as the hope that their collective strength can propel them towards a better future.

Take, for instance, the sisterhood circle of Harriet Tubman and the brave women who supported and guided her on her quest for freedom. This labyrinthine network of formerly enslaved women, dedicated abolitionists, and unyielding supporters constructed the pillars of the Underground Railroad, ensuring the success of its purpose in the face of seemingly insurmountable adversity. Through their collective tenacity, these intrepid women created an unbreakable chain of resilience that shattered the shackles of oppression and set the stage for the monumental struggles that lay ahead.

Fast forward a century, and we find another example of the life-altering impact of sisterhood circles in the Civil Rights Movement: Black women like Fannie Lou Hamer, Ella Baker, and Rosa Parks, who played essential roles in dismantling the suffocating straits of segregation. Embedded within the larger Civil Rights struggle, they also nurtured close-knit circles that fortified the resolve of others and fostered the growth of new generations of activists. Through faith and fellowship, these women tapped into the collective resilience of their shared ancestors, unearthing an unstoppable force that would bring about lasting change for Black people in America.

In today's rapidly changing world, where Black women must grapple with the intersecting challenges posed by shifting global landscapes, their tradition of sisterhood circles remains an enduring source of strength. In the digital age, a new generation of Black women are harnessing the power of technology to create virtual sisterhood circles, connecting with each other across borders and oceans, through platforms like blogs, online forums, and social media groups. Whether their focus is on mental health, entrepreneurship, or artistry, each sisterhood circle adds a unique strand to the tapestry of Black women's communal resilience.

Consider, for instance, the potent force of the Me Too movement, conceptualized by Tarana Burke – a Black woman who dared to break the silence around sexual assault and usher in a tidal wave of global outcry. As women from all walks of life took to social media to share their stories, a powerful sisterhood circle emerged, unified by the collective cry for justice and healing. Through this innovative and far-reaching incarnation of the sisterhood circle, Black women and their allies found strength, support, and empowerment in their shared experiences, galvanized by the courageous voice of their sister who dared to speak truth to power.

As we move forward in time, the importance of sisterhood circles in the lives of Black women remains undiminished. Existing at the nexus of multiple, often complex, identities – Black women are uniquely poised to face challenges that strike at the heart of these intersections. Whether in the realm of education, health, economic opportunity, or social equity, the resilience and ferocity forged in the crucible of sisterhood circles serve as a resonant reminder of the powerful, enduring force of community.

In a world still marred by systemic disparities, prejudice, and ignorance, the nurturing power of sisterhood circles offers an unyielding bulwark against the forces that would seek to break the spirit and trample the dreams of Black women. Existing beyond the coattails of the great heroines who paved the way, the essence of the sisterhood circle remains undiminished: a beacon that calls upon Black women to gather, bond, and support one another, ensuring that the threads of resilience that bind them together – forged over centuries of anguish and struggle – emerge stronger, more vibrant, and more defiant than ever before.

Gullah/Geechee: A Legacy of Resilience and Unity

Nestled in the wind-swept shores of the American South Atlantic coast, stretching from North Carolina down to Northern Florida, lies a remarkable, yet often overlooked, gem of African American historical and cultural heritage: the Gullah/Geechee Nation. This vibrant, resilient community of descendants of enslaved Africans have, against all odds, managed to preserve their distinct language, cultural practices, and folk tales, crafting a unique tapestry of life that embodies the unparalleled resilience, adaptability, and unity of the Black women who have called this land their home for centuries.

The Gullah/Geechee's origins can be traced back to the transatlantic slave trade, when enslaved West Africans – predominantly from the coastal regions of present-day Sierra Leone, Liberia, and Angola – were forcibly transported to the coastal areas of the United States. The ecological and geographical peculiarities of the region, encompassing a vast expanse of marshland, islands, and treacherous coastal waterways, would serve as a catalyst for the enslaved Africans to band together, forging tightly knit communities defined by a staunch, unyielding commitment to mutual support, collaboration, and preservation of their African heritage.

The Gullah/Geechee Nation is a bold, living testament to the transcendent power of unity in the face of adversity, demonstrating the unbreakable bonds of sisterhood that have fortified and sustained Black women throughout history. As the powerful backbone of their communities, the women of the Gullah/Geechee Nation have deftly navigated the dizzying complexities of a world marred by systemic oppression, discrimination, and marginalization, tapping into their ancestral wisdom and fortitude to preserve their culture and enrich the lives of their descendants.

One of the most striking examples of the Gullah/Geechee's unwavering commitment to cultural preservation lies in their language – an enchanting, mellifluous Creole dialect infused with the haunting echoes of their West African forebears. A linguistic embodiment of resilience and resistance, the Gullah language deftly straddles the chasm between Africa and America, giving voice to the indomitable spirit of defiance and adaptability that has characterized Black women's experiences throughout the ages. Embodying the folk wisdom, historical narratives, and lessons carried across the ocean by their ancestors, the Gullah language has been lovingly preserved and transmitted across generations, weaving an unbreakable chain of linguistic resilience that binds the Gullah/Geechee women to both their past and future.

Rising beyond the confines of the spoken word, the indelible spirit of resilience and unity is further evinced in the breathtaking tapestry of unique arts and crafts that the Gullah/Geechee women have lovingly cultivated, utilizing locally sourced materials, such as sweetgrass, palmetto, and longleaf pine needles, to create stunning works of art that reflect their deep connection to both the land and their cultural heritage. Like the intricate stitches of a sweetgrass basket, each strand is woven with unmatched precision, care, and dedication, encompassing and embodying the countless generations of Black women who have emerged from adversity with unwavering determination and strength.

However, the true measure of the Gullah/Geechee Nation's resilience and unity is not found solely in the artistry of their cultural artifacts, nor in the lilting cadence of their language. It is in the unbroken chain of sisterhood and solidarity that has empowered them to rise above countless trials and challenges, standing united in their determination to preserve their fragile, yet fiercely tenacious, heritage. The Gullah/Geechee women, drawing on the collective strength and wisdom of their ancestors, have built and nurtured a vibrant, thriving community that represents a microcosm of the broader tapestry of Black women's lives, illustrating the profound, enduring power of community, collaboration, and sisterhood.

In a world where African American cultural heritage is often sidelined, obscured, or erased entirely, the Gullah/Geechee Nation stands as a shining beacon of hope and defiance, a powerful reminder of the transcendent resilience and unity that define the journey of Black women throughout history. Within the lush, verdant marshlands and whispering, ghostly shores of the American South, the indomitable spirit of the Gullah/Geechee people continues to rise, borne on the wings of sisterhood, solidarity, and an unshakable belief in the power of unity to overcome the trials and tribulations of life.

As we step back from the unforgettable, inspirational story of the Gullah/Geechee Nation and turn our focus towards broader discussions of community in the realm of healing, restorative practices, and traditions, let us not forget the rich, vibrant tapestry of resilience and unity that these remarkable women have so painstakingly woven throughout their history.

Healing Circles: Traditional and Modern Restorative Practices

The transformative power of healing has played a crucial role in the lives of Black women throughout history and beyond, providing a crucial means to foster individual and collective growth, self-discovery, and ultimately, the restoration of community bonds. As Black women have faced various challenges and intersecting adversities, nurturing the mind, body, and spirit has been central to overcoming these obstacles and cultivating resilience. Through restorative practices and healing traditions passed down through generations, Black women have honed the power to face adversity by tapping into their inherent strengths, reclaiming their histories, and recognizing the distinct healing power of their communities.

At the heart of these restorative practices is the fundamental understanding that holistic healing encompasses not only physical well-being but also emotional, psychological, and spiritual wellness. For centuries, Black women have embraced diverse traditions that aim to balance these aspects of their lives, reflecting ancestral wisdom and time-honored methods of fostering mental, emotional, and spiritual restoration. From African-rooted rituals and ceremonies to herbal remedies and the exploration of natural resources, these healing practices embody the essence of Black women's experiences – a living tapestry of blood, sweat, and tears, lovingly woven into the fabric of their collective past and present.

The enduring relevance of these restorative practices is evident in the countless contemporary initiatives and organizations launched or led by Black women to foster community healing. Where systemic inequities and barriers have resulted in unequal access to mental and emotional wellness resources, Black women have taken it upon themselves to address these gaps, creating safe spaces where healing and introspection can ignite radical transformation. Grassroots initiatives such as healing circles, community-based therapy, and workshops designed to empower and enlighten Black women serve as poignant examples of the creative ways in which healing crafts pathways towards self-actualization and self-discovery.

Moreover, the practice of storytelling constitutes a vital tool in the arsenal of restorative practices wielded by Black women. Through the power of narrative, stories of personal and collective suffering, resilience, and triumph are given life - transcending the boundaries of time, space, and geographical location. Rooted in the same ancient oral traditions passed down from one generation to another, storytelling enables Black women to reclaim their histories, honor their ancestors, and recognize the inherent power that lies in the act of giving voice to their experiences.

In addition, the rise of digital platforms and social media has paved the way for a new era in restorative practices amongst Black women. Online forums and virtual networks provide vital outlets for celebrating triumphs, mourning losses, and finding solace in shared experiences. In this brave new world of virtual connection lies an intersection where forgotten healing traditions and burgeoning technological innovations can coalesce, forging a bridge between the wisdom of the past and the promise of the future.

As Black women continue to enact restorative practices and uphold healing traditions, the importance of community healing and resilience cannot be overstated. It is through the alchemy of pain, loss, and hardship that the precious metal of endurance and rebirth can be forged – a testament to the unparalleled resilience of generations of Black women who walked, limped, or crawled to give their descendants the chance to soar. In celebrating and exploring the restorative practices that lift and strengthen their communities, Black women are not only honoring their ancestors but also ensuring that future generations will be empowered by the knowledge and inspiration that invigorates hope, kindles self-discovery, and births resilience.

As the echoes of past struggles reverberate into the present, and the fight for justice and equality continues across the globe, the healing traditions and restorative practices of Black women serve as testimony to the limitless potential of community to sustain, nurture, and galvanize their resilience throughout the ages. Bringing forth the enduring legacy of collective strength in the face of adversity, Black women collaborate in the eternal dance of healing and transformation - united in their unwavering quest to build a world that recognizes, celebrates, and uplifts the vibrant essence and power that springs forth from their ancestral roots.

Grassroots Glory: Black Women Spearheading Change

In the rich, vibrant tapestry of the African American journey, grassroots movements have long been the lifeblood of transformative change, providing crucial impetus for social, political, and economic progress. As stewards of their communities and tireless advocates for a more equitable and just society, Black women have emerged as catalytic leaders in these local initiatives, mobilizing collective power to overcome systemic barriers and dismantle the structures of exclusion that have sidelined and silenced their voices for far too long.

The extraordinary strength, creativity, and resilience of these women have fueled the fires of countless grassroots movements, propelling the needle of change against the relentless tide of adversity. Black women leaders have pioneered unique space-making strategies, harnessing their individual and collective strengths to forge powerful alliances that transcend the boundaries of race, class, and geography, acknowledging the fundamental premise that elevates many grassroots movements: the belief that when one rises, all rise.

One such exemplary luminary of grassroots activism is Fannie Lou Hamer, a determined civil rights activist who fought tirelessly for the right to vote during the early 1960s. Born into a sharecropping family in Mississippi, Hamer faced extreme poverty, intimidation, and violence as she sought to secure voting rights for her community, advocating on behalf of marginalized groups in an era rife with racial constraints. Her tenacity and passion for justice culminated in the founding of the Mississippi Freedom Democratic Party, a true grassroots movement dedicated to achieving political representation for black citizens. Hamer's unrelenting spirit serves as a powerful testament to the transformative potential of grassroots initiatives led by Black women.

In the world of educational access and activism, Marva Collins, a teacher, and educator, emerged as a pathbreaking figure, driven by her unwavering belief in the power of education to uplift and empower the African American community. With sheer determination and limited resources, Collins founded Westside Preparatory School in Chicago, a school that would become renowned for its ability to inspire and educate low-income African American children whom many deemed "unteachable." Igniting a revolution at the heart of the education system, Collins demonstrated the extraordinary potential of grassroots initiatives driven by compassionate, resilient Black women.

Beyond the realms of political and educational activism, Black women have also been pivotal in harnessing the transformative power of local organizing to address health inequities within their communities. Emblematic of these grassroots health advocacy initiatives is the work of Hazel Dukes, the dynamic president of the NAACP of New York and former director of the Harlem Hospital Center. Through her unwavering commitment to community-based health advocacy, Dukes sought to improve healthcare access, affordability, and quality for African Americans in her community. The impact of her sustained, impassioned efforts can be felt in every corner of the Harlem community.

In the present day, Black women continue to lead groundbreaking grassroots movements in diverse spheres of life. The co-founder of the Black Lives Matter Global Network, Patrisse Cullors, has played a vital role in mobilizing global resistance against racial injustice and systemic oppression, galvanizing the world to confront the deeply rooted and pervasive inequalities that disproportionately target Black communities. A visionary who has ignited global discourse, Cullors exemplifies the monumental power of grassroots organizing in shaping the course of history.

Grassroots movements, deeply embedded within the fabric of the African American experience, are the conduits of change, the wellsprings of hope, and the crucibles of innovation that propel the journey towards a more equitable, inclusive world. Through their visionary leadership, unyielding courage, and the fierce tenacity that has come to define the essence of Black womanhood, these remarkable trailblazers have harnessed the transformative potential of grassroots organizing, transcending geographical, cultural, and socio-economic divides to bring about meaningful change within their communities.

As we examine the myriad ways in which Black women have shaped and transformed the world through their grassroots initiatives, we glean invaluable insights into the unparalleled power of community-driven, direct action – lessons that serve as a clarion call to action for future generations of Black women leaders. Through the monumental legacies of women like Hamer, Collins, Dukes, and Cullors, we bear witness to the boundless potential of grassroots organizing to not only give voice to the marginalized but to topple the structures of power that have long stifled the march towards justice, equity, and freedom.

In this spirit, we embrace the call to nurture the seeds of grassroots movements within our communities, recognizing that each act of defiance, each voice raised in protest, and each hand extended in solidarity contribute to the flourishing of a vibrant, diverse garden of change. As we cultivate and nurture this ever-expanding world, we do so rooted in the knowledge that it is from the fertile soil of grassroots initiatives that the most profound and lasting transformations arise – a testament to the indomitable force of Black women's resilience, vision, and determined action to create a better future for their descendants.

Bridging Generations: The Power of Mentorship

The journey of the Black woman has been one of great trials, but also one of immense strength and purpose. Confronted with seemingly insurmountable challenges and barriers, the resilience and tenacity of Black women throughout history have served as both an inspiration and a guiding light for those who follow in their footsteps. One of the most powerful ways in which this legacy of strength and determination is perpetuated is through mentoring and generational support, a cornerstone of growth and resilience within the African American community.

Mentoring, at its core, is the act of guiding and nurturing a younger person or less experienced individual in order for them to learn, grow, and bring their unique gifts to the world. It is a powerful intergenerational exchange of wisdom, experience, and love – a bridge that connects the past to the present and paves the way for the future. For Black women, the act of mentoring has forged a vital lifeline to their ancestral roots and has proven instrumental in the transmission of values, skills, and life lessons – ensuring that the legacy of strength, resilience, and compassion is carried forward to the next generation.

One compelling example of mentoring and generational support within the context of the Black women's experience can be found in the relationship between "Big Momma" and her grandchildren. In African American families, the figure of "Big Momma" holds a prominent place, often representing the matriarch who has accumulated a wealth of life experience, insight, and wisdom. Her role within the family is to share these invaluable lessons with her children and grandchildren, providing guidance and support to ensure their growth and resilience. Through quiet conversations, family gatherings, or simply by leading by example, "Big Momma" provides the linchpin that holds the family together and instills within her progeny a shared sense of identity, purpose, and belonging.

This uniquely African American form of mentoring also extends to the professional sphere, bestowing a rich tradition of intergenerational mentorship among Black women in a variety of fields and endeavors. From the academic setting, where role models like Zora Neale Hurston, Toni Morrison, and Angela Davis paved the way for countless Black women scholars, to the political arena, where trailblazers like Shirley Chisholm and Barbara Jordan broke down barriers and mentored a new generation of Black women leaders, the legacy of mentorship and generational support has served as a vital vehicle through which Black women continue to thrive and leave indelible marks on the world.

Moreover, the contemporary landscape of mentoring and generational support within the African American community has been uniquely shaped by the rise of digital technologies and social media platforms. Online forums, blogs, and websites dedicated to promoting the growth and success of Black women have flourished in recent years, providing a wealth of resources, support networks, and opportunities for intergenerational connection. This new frontier of digital mentorship serves as an innovative means through which the wisdom and experience of older generations can be shared with younger individuals, empowering and uplifting them.

Yet, the role of mentoring and generational support within the Black women's experience is not confined to a one-way transfer of wisdom and advice. Rather, it is a symbiotic exchange that acknowledges and celebrates the unique perspectives, talents, and insights that each generation brings to the table. As Black women continue to forge new paths, defy stereotypes, and shatter conventional expectations, they offer innovative visions to uplift and strengthen their communities – enriching the tapestry of mentorship with the brilliance of their collective achievements.

In this crucible of resilience, nurtured through the potent alchemy of mentoring and generational support, the Black woman's spirit blazes forth undimmed, illuminating the world with her indomitable courage, strength, and wisdom. As the torch is passed from one generation to another, the flame of Black women's hearts kindles yet more brilliant sparks, setting the stage for an even more luminous and triumphant future. For, as has been so eloquently observed by Zora Neale Hurston, a trailblazing Black woman author and anthropologist who served as a mentor to future generations of Black women intellectuals: "I am not tragically colored. There is no great sorrow dammed up in my soul, nor lurking behind my eyes ... I do not mind at all. I do not weep at the world ... I am too busy sharpening my oyster knife."

Together We Rise: Building Stronger Communities

One such pillar of community empowerment revolves around the establishment of safe, nurturing spaces that serve as hubs for Black women to gather, share their experiences, and invest in each other's growth and well-being. These spaces have taken various forms, ranging from church gatherings to quilting circles, book clubs, and hair salons. In these settings, Black women are free to engage in open, honest conversations about the challenges they face, creating an environment of empathy and understanding that paves the way for collective healing and growth. Significantly, these spaces also serve as important arenas for the cultivation of important life skills, as women learn from one another in practical domains such as financial management, personal wellness, and political participation.

Another crucial element of community empowerment among Black women lies in the mobilization of collective resources to address pressing concerns and challenges that affect their lives. Through the establishment of mutual aid societies, cooperatives, and neighborhood organizations, Black women have been able to pool their financial, social, and intellectual capital to address issues such as access to affordable housing, healthcare, and education. For instance, the Black Women's Health Imperative, founded in 1983 by a group of visionary Black women, has focused on addressing health disparities within their community through a host of programs, advocacy efforts, and partnerships. This collective approach to problem-solving underscores the immense capacity of Black women to come together for the common good, embracing the power that lies in their unity as they confront and dismantle structures of marginalization and injustice.

In harnessing the power of community empowerment, Black women have also embraced the transformative potential of storytelling, integrating oral traditions, historical narratives, and personal experiences to create a rich tapestry of shared heritage that transcends individual struggle. Storytelling allows Black women to reclaim their history, bear witness to the triumphs and tragedies of their predecessors, and acknowledge the strength inherent in their collective identity. As women share their stories, they create connections, affirming their belonging within a community emboldened by the knowledge that no challenge is insurmountable when they join forces.

Moreover, the role of mentorship and intergenerational support in the African American community has been a fundamental component of community empowerment, fostering the growth of future leaders and instilling in them a sense of commitment to the collective. Through mentorship programs, outreach initiatives, and educational efforts, older generations of Black women share the wisdom of their experiences, nurturing the dreams and aspirations of their younger counterparts. These intergenerational connections create a synergistic feedback loop, allowing generations of Black women to learn from one another's successes and failures and build upon the foundations of their forebears.

In light of these myriad strategies and practices, the significance of community empowerment within the Black women's experience becomes strikingly clear. By fortifying the bonds that unite them, nurturing spaces for growth and learning, pooling collective resources, and investing in the leaders of tomorrow, Black women have harnessed the transformative energy and resources embedded in the community. This potent force of unyielding strength and determination empowers and uplifts not just the individual but also the entire community, offering a rich model for the boundless potential of collective action in the struggle for justice, equity, and opportunity.

LEGACY OF TRIUMPH: OVERCOMING ADVERSITY TOGETHER

In the timeless words of Maya Angelou, "You may encounter many defeats, but you must not be defeated." This powerful sentiment, grounded in the experiences and triumphs of Black women throughout history, serves as a testament to their unwavering resilience in the face of adversity. Though each generation has encountered a unique set of struggles and hardships, Black women have endeavored to persevere, uplifting one another and forging pathways to overcome the seemingly insurmountable challenges before them. The navigation of these adversities has often occurred through the cultivation of collaborative bonds and intergenerational mentorship, empowering Black women to achieve remarkable feats of personal strength and success even when the odds seemed stacked against them.

In tracing the lineage of overcoming adversity within the African American community, it can be instructive to consider a pivotal moment in American history: the Civil Rights Movement. For many Black women, this was a tumultuous time marked by immense personal struggle, as they fought valiantly to claim the rights and recognition that were long overdue. Despite the perils of engaging in activism and asserting their humanity on this contentious battleground, these heroines found solace and strength in the wisdom, guidance, and bravery of those who had come before them. In the stories of courageous women like Ida B. Wells, Harriet Tubman, and Sojourner Truth, they discovered a legacy of resilience that imbued them with the fortitude to tackle the injustices they faced head-on and pursue a better future for themselves and their children.

For some of this brave cohort, adversity took the shape of racial segregation and the violent backlash against integration efforts. Here, Rosa Parks serves as a shining example of a woman undeterred by the forces of hatred that sought to marginalize her. Parks' quiet act of defiance in refusing to yield her seat on a Montgomery bus not only ignited a catalyst for the larger Civil Rights Movement but also provided a meaningful symbol of resistance for generations of Black women to come. While her single act was but a small victory in the grand scheme of racially-driven injustice, Parks' refusal to submit to the yoke of oppression demonstrated the immense power of individual courage and conviction in overcoming systemic barriers. Crucially, through her steadfast determination in the face of adversity, she would go on to inspire thousands of men and women alike to join the struggle for justice and equality.

Another powerful example of overcoming adversity throughout the generations can be seen in the realm of education. Historically, Black women have faced numerous obstacles in their quest for self-improvement and intellectual growth, including unequal access to quality schooling and resources, overt racism, and patriarchal attitudes that sought to constrain their ambitions. Yet, time and again, these trailblazers defied conventional expectations, finding solace in the pursuit of knowledge and rubbing shoulders with the great minds of their generations. For example, Mary McLeod Bethune and Annie Turnbo Malone both faced limited access to education growing up, but they went on to become highly successful and influential figures renowned for their impact on their communities. Both women also created myriad opportunities for others, leveraging their success to establish educational institutions, orphanages, social programs, and philanthropic efforts that would serve as launching pads for others to achieve greatness – emboldening their students and beneficiaries to believe in the vastness of their potential despite the constraints imposed upon them by societal prejudices.

In more recent times, the resilience and tenacity of Black women as they navigate adversity can be seen in the realm of the professional world. Often faced with glass ceilings and discouraging statistics, Black women have charged forward to break down barriers in the most competitive spheres – from politics and law to the sciences and the arts. This progress, achieved in the face of systemic obstacles such as wage gaps, underrepresentation, and discriminatory practices, has been a testament to their determination and capacity to support one another through the exchange of mentorship, encouragement, and advocacy. By celebrating the accomplishments of trailblazers like Michelle

Obama, Oprah Winfrey, and Mae Jemison, Black women have demonstrated the indomitable strength that lies in refusing to accept defeat and daring to succeed in spite of the odds.

Passing Down Resilience: Lessons From Our Elders

As the sun rises on the horizon, casting its light on the vast tapestry of human history, there are countless stories that remain untold, obscured by the shadows of neglect and misrepresentation. Among these myriad narratives, the landscape of adversity faced by Black women throughout history is an indelible testament to their unwavering resilience, strength, and sheer determination in the face of innumerable obstacles. To contemplate the historic context of these struggles is not an exercise in dwelling on the negative or amplifying suffering but rather a necessary act of acknowledging the irrefutable power of Black women – the audacity with which they refused to be silenced, the defiance they embodied to transcend and transform the barriers set before them, and the triumphs that emerged from the crucibles of tribulation.

Moreover, these historic struggles exist not merely in the realm of physical subjugation but also traverse the contours of psychological and emotional oppression. The tools of racism and sexism have been wielded with sinister precision against Black women, negating their worth and eroding their confidence in their own abilities and contributions to society. This vicious onslaught has manifested in various dimensions, such as the simultaneous exclusion and objectification of Black women in popular culture, the erasure of their voices and perspectives in art and literature, and the systematic minimization of their presence in fields such as the sciences, politics, and the academy. This landscape of marginalization has engendered a complex interplay between the external impressions imposed upon Black women and their innermost perceptions of self, creating a relentless battle for self-identity and emancipation from the chains of oppressive stereotypes.

In addition to these existential struggles, the historical context of adversity also encompasses the countless material challenges faced by

Black women daily, from access to healthcare, education, and housing to confronting the dangers of violence and discrimination that persist in contemporary society. These practical dimensions of adversity not only underscore the tenacity and strength required to navigate life as a Black woman in a world riddled with inequality and prejudice but also illuminate the boundless potential that lies within each individual – the unwavering will to persevere and rise above even the bleakest of circumstances.

However, this landscape of adversity is not an unbroken expanse of darkness, devoid of hope and resistance. Rather, it is punctuated by moments of incredible triumph, as Black women have continued to overcome the barriers erected to keep them constrained, subverting the expectations of a society that sought to diminish and discredit their power. In the face of these daunting odds, Black women have always found ways to defy the limitations imposed upon them, crafting legacies of success, leadership, and innovation that attest to their extraordinary resilience. As we contemplate this historic landscape of adversity, it is essential that we also bear witness to these moments of transcendence, recognizing the capacity of Black women to reclaim their destiny and shape the course of history, despite the forces that sought to oppose them.

As the sun sets upon the panorama of history, casting its dusky hues across the landscape of adversity faced by Black women, we remain deeply cognizant of the incredible strength and courage that have defined their journey. Recognizing these triumphs of resilience and empowerment forms an essential cornerstone in the ongoing struggle for justice, equality, and the full realization of the potential that lies dormant within the heart of every Black woman. By illuminating the darkness of adversity and drawing forth the profound wisdom and fortitude preserved within these stories, we may yet behold a future where the voices and contributions of Black women will hold their rightful place of honor – a testament to their indomitable spirit in the face of seemingly insurmountable challenges.

As Black women continue to rise alongside the luminaries who graced their histories, let us hold onto the truth that adversity breeds strength, and the landscape of struggle gives birth to the potential for boundless transcendence and undaunted resilience.

Standing Tall: Stories of Courage and Victory

Throughout history, Black women have developed a rich tapestry of strategies and coping mechanisms to navigate adversity and foster resilience. Passed down from generation to generation, these tools have served as lifelines, guiding the hands of countless heroines while providing solace in the most challenging of circumstances. As we delve deeper into this wealth of generational wisdom, we uncover the ingenious ways in which Black women have adapted, thrived, and overcome despite the tumultuous cards life has dealt them.

In examining these key strategies and coping mechanisms, we must begin by understanding the critical role played by oral traditions in conveying this generational wisdom. In African societies, the preservation and sharing of history, beliefs, and life lessons were anchored in the art of storytelling. Griots, or gifted storytellers, were revered for their ability to convey the wisdom of ancestors through captivating narratives. Black women, weavers of tales, nurtured young girls by passing on their own experiences and those of their forebears, imbuing them with the courage and knowledge necessary to withstand life's trials. Through richly textured stories, dispersing laughter even in the face of tribulation, these women taught their daughters, sisters, and friends the strength of sisterhood, the value of perseverance, and above all, the unparalleled power of their own resilient spirits.

Understanding the body as a vessel and the soul as its keeper, Black women across generations also recognized the importance of self-care as a coping mechanism. Embodied through communal rituals such as hair braiding, communal baths, and the preparation of traditional herbal remedies, these practices fostered a sense of unity and shared experience. Even amidst the cruel and inhuman conditions of chattel slavery, Black women risked their lives to maintain these vital sources of solace sand healing. As the shackles of bondage fell away, the significance of these shared rituals persisted, providing a wellspring of strength and comfort to those facing racial and gender-based discrimination in a still-divided world.

Another vital coping mechanism embraced by generations of Black women is the role of faith and spirituality. Through prayer, meditation, and other spiritual practices, Black women have sought refuge and guidance in their unyielding belief in a higher power. Drawing on a rich history of African cosmology, as well as syncretic faiths such as Vodou and Santería that emerged in the African diaspora, these spiritual practices have offered Black women a unique form of solace and connection. In engaging with spiritual practices, these women have forged relationships with ancestors, embraced their spiritual gifts, and discovered a deeper sense of purpose – providing them with a resilience beyond measure.

The enduring strength of Black women can also be attributed to their determination to succeed in the face of adversity. Despite the constraints imposed by a society that sought to marginalize them, Black women have displayed remarkable fortitude in their pursuit of education, professional opportunities, and personal growth. The legacy of these trailblazers has fueled successive generations, illustrating the value of refusing to be constrained by others' expectations. By defying the odds through perseverance and tenacity, Black women have forged an enduring example of resilience, demonstrating to future generations that success is not only possible but inevitable when one stays true to their purpose.

Undeniably, the concept of sisterhood has formed the bedrock of support and empowerment for Black women throughout history. Solidarity and community engagement have resulted in the establishment of various organizations, philanthropic initiatives, and mentorship programs – all aimed at uplifting the voices and experiences of Black women. In the spirit of sisterhood, these collective efforts harness the vibrancy of Black women's resilience, providing safe spaces and opportunities to share, learn, and grow. United, these communities exemplify the formidable force of Black women supporting one another in their diverse journeys towards personal and collective success.

As we embrace the kaleidoscopic beauty and fortitude of generational wisdom, it is essential to acknowledge the ever-evolving strategies and coping mechanisms that Black women have employed for centuries. This understanding deepens our appreciation of the resilience demonstrated by these heroines, connecting the past with the present and forging a bridge to a future where Black women may continue to embody their indomitable spirits. The tapestry of generational wisdom illuminates not only the challenges these women have faced but also the triumphs they have achieved. For future generations of Black women, it is through the lens of these ancestral legacies that they can begin to envision and embrace their own unique paths, becoming the embodiment of resilience for generations still unborn.

Forward Ever: Black Women Paving the Way

The indomitable spirit of Black women throughout history finds itself manifest in the myriad stories of resilience and triumph that grace the tapestry of their collective experience. While adversity has taken many forms throughout the ages, the unwavering resolve of these individuals persisted, channeled into myriad acts of defiance, survival, and reinvention that eschew the constraints of their circumstances. Through these examples, we bear witness to the power of resilience when wielded across generations and within diverse layers of society.

Consider the remarkable case of Elizabeth "MumBet" Freeman, a woman born into slavery on the eve of the American Revolution. A keen observer, Freeman's inherent intelligence, and resourcefulness led her to study the law. Consequently, she learned of the newly enacted Massachusetts state constitution, which declared that "all are born free and equal." With this knowledge, Freeman enlisted the help of a local lawyer to sue for freedom and ultimately triumphed. Freeman's victory did not just secure her own emancipation; it set a precedent for the abolition of slavery throughout Massachusetts, thereby ushering in an era of change that defied the status quo. Her resilience shattered the chains of bondage, forever altering the course of history.

As we move into the twentieth century, we encounter Claudette Colvin, a teenage girl whose act of defiance sparked a chain of events that culminated in the Civil Rights Movement. In Montgomery, Alabama, a young Colvin refused to relinquish her seat on a segregated bus in 1955, igniting a flame of resistance to racial segregation. Despite her valiant action, Colvin found herself overshadowed by the poignant figure of Rosa Parks months later, a harbinger of the civil rights movement that was poised to sweep the nation. Nonetheless, Colvin's resilience in the face of adversity, both societal and personal, served as a potent illustration of the strength of will that pervades the spirit of Black women.

In an entirely different sphere, we witness the resilience of Black women in the exceptional story of the "Hidden Figures" of NASA. Katherine Johnson, along with her colleagues Dorothy Vaughan and Mary Jackson, were Black female mathematicians whose vital work contributed to some of NASA's most significant space missions, yet until recently, their stories remained confined to the margins of history. These trailblazing women overcame adversity through intelligence, rigor, and determination, achieving remarkable results despite entrenched racial and gender-based discrimination. With the publication of Margot Shetterly's book and the subsequent film adaptation, their resilience and insurmountable achievements are now finally receiving their rightful acknowledgment.

One more example of transformative resilience is the story of Tarana Burke, a social activist and community organizer who created the "Me Too" Movement in 2006. Originally devised as a grassroots campaign to empower survivors of sexual harassment and assault within underprivileged communities of color, the movement soon gained global traction, emerging as a powerful cultural force that sought to dismantle pervasive attitudes towards sexual violence and hold perpetrators accountable. Burke's resilience and unwavering commitment to her cause have not only offered solace for millions of survivors but also triggered a seismic shift in social consciousness and the pursuit of justice for Black women worldwide.

These exemplary case studies encapsulate the very essence of resilience in action – a testament to the boundless fortitude and courage demonstrated by generations of Black women throughout history. As we delve deeper into these rich narratives, we uncover a wellspring of inspiration, furnishing hope in the face of adversity, and evidence of the power of the resilient spirit to overcome seemingly insurmountable challenges and change the world.

The sun's fading light casts long shadows across the landscape of resilience, illuminating the magnitude and diversity of the achievements of Black women who overcame adversity. Their stories not only inspire but evoke a sense of awe and humility, along with an understanding that the lineage of resilience continues to thrive in the veins of present and future generations. By acknowledging and honoring the irrefutable power of these women, we not only reshape the narrative of Black women's history but also pave the way for forthcoming generations to claim their inherited capacity to transcend adversity and build an indelible legacy of their own.

Seeds for Tomorrow: Cultivating Hope and Strength

The legacy of resilience, glimpsed in the myriad anecdotes that have emerged throughout history, continue to define the experiences of today's Black women in a world that is continually fraught with challenges and setbacks. As each generation is confronted by different manifestations of adversity, the resilience that has been weaved into the tapestry of Black women's lived experiences equips them with the fortitude and determination to redefine the boundaries of possibility and persist in the face of opposition. Through the examination of the lives of contemporary women, we observe the strategies and coping mechanisms deployed to overcome adversity and, ultimately, thrive and shatter expectations.

Perhaps one of the most salient examples of resilience in recent times is the ascent of the iconic figure of Kamala Harris, the first woman of African and South Asian descent to be elected as the Vice President of the United States. Despite the seemingly insurmountable barriers erected by generations of systemic racism and gender bias, Harris's trajectory into the upper echelons of global politics brandishes the indomitable spirit of resilience embodied by her predecessors. Her success is not merely a testament to her personal attributes; it signifies a broader victory for Black women, engendering a ripple effect that inspires and galvanizes communities worldwide.

Alongside the realm of politics, Black women continually break barriers within the world of sports, transforming the norms and expectations in traditionally male-dominated arenas. Serena Williams, a beacon of clinical talent and fierce determination, represents the embodiment of resilience. Her prodigious achievements in the world of tennis have dismantled the racial and gender stereotypes that sought to curtail her and her contemporaries. Within the narratives of these remarkable women, we witness the power of resilience in action, as we see them maneuver through prejudice, criticism, and personal adversity, emerging as icons of inspiration for generations to come.

Beyond the spheres of politics and sports, the resilience of today's Black women is also evident in the domains of literature and the arts. Writers such as Chimamanda Ngozi Adichie, Ta-Nehisi Coates, and Roxane Gay, among others, have forged their unique perspectives and experiences into prose that not only resonate but challenge readers to confront the realities of race, gender, and identity. Through their work, these authors are forging new paths for representation and expanding the parameters of intellectual discourse, cultivating spaces where Black women's resilience can be celebrated and embraced.

Similarly, in the realm of entertainment, Black women, such as Ava DuVernay, Lena Waithe, and Issa Rae, have not only defied expectation but have also crafted new pathways for emerging creatives. These women, as filmmakers, producers, writers, and performers, have harnessed their talents and resilience to shape narratives that uplift Black women and provide platforms for nuanced portrayals previously stifled by racism and sexism. Their success, much like their predecessors, evidences the profound impact of resilience in shaping the lives and artistic contributions of Black women.

As we turn our attention to the realm of entrepreneurship, we encounter myriad instances of Black women surmounting the obstacles of an often-unaccommodating world to thrive in spaces that have historically excluded them. Black female business owners such as Richelieu Dennis, founder of Shea Moisture, exemplify the resourcefulness and tenacity required to flourish in competitive environments, bolstered by a keen understanding of their communities and a dedication to empowering them.

In recognizing and celebrating the legacy of resilience that courses through the veins of Black women today, we acknowledge the debt owed to the generations who have come before — the women who not only fought against adversity but transformed their experiences into a wellspring of strength and wisdom. It is the indomitable spirit of these trailblazers that has sparked the fires of determination and talent in the hearts of the women who have followed in their footsteps, as contemporary Black women embrace their heritage of resilience, forge new paths, and allow their strength to scribe the cultural narrative of the future.

As we reflect on the stunning examples of resilience and triumph that permeate the lives of Black women today, we are reminded that the journey is one that traverses the span of generations. As each new cohort of women makes their mark within the annals of history, they contribute to the continuous unfolding of the tapestry of resilience, offering inspiration, solace, and guidance to those who will come after them. Drawing upon the enduring narratives of their ancestors, these women are simultaneously shaping a vibrant legacy of success and fortitude that will fortify future generations in their efforts to realize their full potential in a world that, slowly but surely, is beginning to expand its horizons.

RECLAIMING OUR NARRATIVES: THE POWER OF OUR STORIES

Throughout history, the indomitable spirit of resilience and determination found in the hearts of Black women has been pivotal in shaping the course of their communities and the wider world. As generations have risen to confront and transcend the diverse range of adversities that marked their respective eras, the lessons derived from their experiences have been meticulously woven into a tapestry that not only bestows inspiration but serves as a blueprint for future generations. This legacy - brimming with wisdom, courage, and tenacity - is ripe with lessons that contemporary Black women can glean from in their pursuit of personal and collective growth. It is within this rich trove of knowledge that future generations can find solace, encouragement, and the impetus to forge ahead, emboldened by the enduring strength of their foremothers.

One of the most profound lessons gleaned from generations past is the resolve to remain undeterred in the face of adversity, regardless of form or magnitude. This unwavering fortitude, exemplified in the defiant acts of the Bus Boycott-era activists and the trailblazing mathematical prowess of NASA's Hidden Figures, underscores the importance of persisting in the face of opposition. It is this relentless determination that enables the descendants of these resilient women to confront the unique challenges of their era, armed with the knowledge that the strength of their ancestors courses through their veins. These lessons in resilience serve as a clarion call for future generations, imbuing them with the confidence and courage to transcend the boundaries of their circumstances and redefine the parameters of possibility.

Moreover, the invaluable insights derived from past generations reveal the significance of embracing one's identity and remaining true to oneself, regardless of societal expectations or imposed stereotypes. The meteoric rise of cultural icons such as Serena Williams, Chimamanda Ngozi Adichie, and Kamala Harris is predicated upon their unwavering commitment to shatter expectations and forge their distinctive paths. In doing so, these women have imparted a vital message to future generations: that the nuanced tapestry of Black womanhood is a source of strength and inspiration, not a hindrance to be concealed or overcome. It is in the celebration of these lived experiences that contemporary women can draw inspiration, allowing their individuality to inform their endeavors and invigorate their pursuits.

Further, the legacy of previous generations imparts the crucial importance of cultivating and nurturing community ties as a means of fostering growth, empowerment, and resilience. The sisterhood circles, grassroots movements, and mentoring initiatives that have blossomed through time stand testament to the power of communal cohesion and the transformative potential of collective action. For future generations, these insights offer a beacon of guidance, illuminating the necessity for collaboration, support, and togetherness in order to manifest change and transcend adversity. Through the lessons of their predecessors, young Black women can appreciate the power immanent in their communities and harness this strength to propel their dreams and ambitions to fruition.

The storied history of Black women's resilience is not merely a chronicle of the past; it is a living legacy that continues to breathe life and vigor into the aspirations and pursuits of generations to come. The lessons derived from the countless examples of courage, tenacity, and triumph that fill the tapestry of Black women's collective experience are an indelible resource that, when harnessed, can guide the footsteps of future trailblazers. As new cohorts emerge, poised to conquer the unique landscape of their era, they do so fortified by the wisdom of their forebears and emboldened by the palpable conviction that the spirit of resilience is an inexorable force within their grasp.

As we consider the wealth of knowledge and inspiration bequeathed to future generations by the tenacious and courageous women who carve their legacies into the annals of history, we are reminded of our duty to uphold their values and emulate their tireless perseverance. It is incumbent upon us to remain steadfast in our pursuit of progress, truth, and unity, so that the essence of resilience may continue to reverberate across the generations that follow. By embracing the lessons of our ancestors and the indomitable spirit that defines us, we ensure that the flame of resilience will continue to burn brightly, illuminating the path of future generations, and offering them the courage to chart their own course toward a world that recognizes, celebrates, and embraces the boundless potential of Black women.

Reflections on the Past: Examining the Strength and Resilience of Ancestors

Weaving through the tapestry of human history are threads of remarkable resilience and strength, particularly emblematic of the lived experiences of Black women. Indeed, it would be remiss not to consider the profound impact of the legacy left by our ancestors, who have bequeathed to us not only a treasure trove of wisdom and knowledge but also an indelible example of tenacity, courage, and grace in the face of adversities, both seen and unseen.

The lives of these forbearers are striking examples of overcoming adversity through grit and determination. But these legacies are more than just a chronicle of the past. They are an enduring reminder that the spirit of resilience runs deep and strong within our veins, continuously inspiring and driving us forward. As we tread along the path carved by our ancestors, we pay homage to their contributions and strive to honor their sacrifices, thereby imbuing our present journey with purpose and meaning.

One such trailblazer is Harriet Tubman, the renowned conductor of the Underground Railroad. Born into the harrowing, abject world of slavery, Tubman demonstrated an unyielding determination to liberate herself and her people from their chains. By courageously defying the expectations of her time and refusing to submit to the forces of oppression, Tubman traversed the treacherous landscape of the antebellum era with a fierce sense of duty and a steadfast commitment to justice. Her tireless advocacy for freedom and equality serves as a shining testament to the staying power of the human spirit, and her legacy of resilience continues to stoke the fires of change within our hearts today.

In the realm of science, the indomitable spirit of resilience echoes through generations with the story of Katherine Johnson, Dorothy Vaughan, and Mary Jackson—NASA's "Hidden Figures." Their unparalleled prowess in mathematical calculations and their brilliant minds played a significant role in the United States' pioneering space missions. In doing so, they transcended the boundaries of race and gender that sought to contain them and, in turn, expanded the horizon of possibility for the young Black girls who would follow in their footsteps. The resilience of these phenomenal women demonstrates that the more significant the challenge, the greater the opportunity for growth and triumph.

Embarking on a voyage into the annals of history, we come across countless examples of the indomitable spirit of resilience, from the indelible influence of Sojourner Truth in the abolitionist and suffragette movements to the unwavering mettle of Rosa Parks and Fannie Lou Hamer in the tumultuous struggle for civil rights. These extraordinary women, in their defiance and determination, have not only transformed the course of history but have also established a legacy of unyielding fortitude that we can draw upon in our own battles.

As we look back on the lives and achievements of these monumental figures, we are reminded of the intrinsic power of resilience and the transformative potential that lies within our grasp. In recognizing and celebrating the strength of our ancestors, we harness the energy cultivated by their experiences and convert it into a force for good, propelling ourselves and our communities forward along the road to progress. Thus, reflecting on the past is, in essence, a testament to our collective memory and an indomitable force that binds us together through time.

Just as the roots of a tree draw sustenance from the soil, we, too, derive strength and wisdom from our ancestors—those resilient, trailblazing women who have left an indelible mark upon the landscape of history. We honor the sacrifices and triumphs of these remarkable women by embracing our heritage, by harnessing the indomitable spirit of resilience, and by perpetuating the cycle of empowerment, growth, and hope. As we continue on our journey, we pay heed to the lessons of the past and strive to carry the torch, blazing a trail for the generations that will follow, ensuring that the spirit of resilience will continue to illuminate the path forward and shape the inexorable course of history. In the rising voices and indelible legacies of our ancestors, we glimpse the reality of our strength—resilience as indomitable as the human spirit itself, a testament to the fierce determination that has driven, and will continue to drive, the vibrant tapestry of Black women's history.

Reclaiming History: Learning from the Stories and Achievements of Unsung Heroines

Throughout history, countless unsung heroines have persisted in the shadows, their names and stories conspicuously absent from the annals of time. These women, their achievements obscured by an insidious blend of prejudice and neglect, recede into the margins of society, leaving their contributions unrecognized and their memories, ephemeral. However, the increasing awareness of their accomplishments and the reclamation of their histories has illuminated not only the resilience and strength of these women, but also the transformative power of rectifying historical omissions and embracing the legacies of those who came before us.

The yearning to learn from these unsung heroines and their stories is more than a historical exercise; it represents an urgent need to acknowledge the strength and ingenuity of our foremothers, to carry their legacy with us, and to empower future generations with their stories. As we strive to unearth the obscured narratives of Black women across time, we discover the rich trove of wisdom and knowledge they have bequeathed to us, their chronicles of endurance and perseverance a testament to the indomitable spirit that echoes across the generations.

Consider, for instance, the groundbreaking work of Dr. Susan McKinney Steward, the first Black female physician in New York State and the third in the United States. Her unwavering commitment to her education, her tireless service to her community, and her pioneering foray into a field that was predominantly white and male is a testament to her profound resilience and formidable fortitude. Despite her trailblazing accomplishments in the world of medicine and her enduring impact on healthcare access for Black communities, her story has remained shrouded in obscurity, known by few and celebrated by even fewer.

Another figure who surges forth from the annals of time is the indefatigable Bessie Coleman, the first Black woman to hold a pilot's license and an erstwhile icon in the primarily white, male-dominated world of early 20th-century aviation. Her relentless pursuit of her dreams—flying all the way to France to complete her training when she was denied access to American flight schools—and her desire to inspire others mark her story as one of vigor and tenacity, fueled by an indomitable spirit that ultimately cost her life. In the soaring arc of Coleman's time in the skies, we can perceive the unfettered essence of resilience and the intrepid determination that still resonates within the hearts of contemporary Black women.

These stories, along with countless others, have been painstakingly excavated from the depths of the past, illuminating the legacies of the extraordinary yet overlooked Black women who prevail at the fringes of history. As we uncover these narratives, we are not only shedding light on their lives and achievements, but also nurturing our own connections to our ancestors and bolstering our sense of identity, strength, and resilience. When we learn of the heroines who defied expectations and transcended the confines of their time, we are reminded that their brilliance still blossoms within us, their spirits of resistance and empowerment propelling us forward to break boundaries and shatter expectations.

The reclamation of these hidden histories describes a journey that is both profound and deeply visceral, a course that leads us into the heart of the labyrinth of our ancestors, where we encounter the echoes of their resilience, the reverberations of their strength, and the subtle whispers of their wisdom. As we trace the paths of these unsung heroines and the indelible marks they have left upon the tapestry of history, we are not only reconciling our connections to the past, but also forging a more vibrant, equitable, and truthful future. By acknowledging and celebrating the achievements of those who have come before us, we create a legacy of resilience and strength that is worthy of inheriting by the generations of Black women who are yet to come.

Ultimately, the process of reclaiming the stories and achievements of unsung heroines is a journey of empowerment, love, and healing—a resolute assertion of our identity, our histories, and the indomitable spirits that connect us across time and space. In elevating the memories of these extraordinary women, we rekindle the flame of resilience that has long fueled our collective progress and remind ourselves that, despite the shadows cast by history, our voices, our stories, and our legacy will forever endure. As we turn the pages, unearthing the rich and varied chronicles of the women who came before us, we lay the foundation for a future in which the voices of Black women ring loud, true, and unapologetic, capturing the essence of the indomitable spirit that has persevered through generations, and illuminating, with fervor and clarity, the powerful and profound resilience that binds us all.

Nurturing Future Leaders: Cultivating Empowerment, Knowledge, and Self-Expression in the Next Generation

As the sun emerges from behind the clouds, casting a glow upon the verdant landscape, the seeds, which have lain dormant beneath the earth, begin to stir and awaken. Nourished by the life-sustaining nutrients from their ancestors and buoyed by their innate potential, these germinating seeds embark on their own journey of growth and discovery. The stories of strength and resilience that we can mine from the depths of our hearts are much like these scarce seeds—endowed with the capacity to flourish and transform the landscape of possibility for the generations yet to come. Indeed, nurturing future leaders is akin to the cultivation of these seeds, fostering an environment of empowerment, knowledge, and self-expression, which allows these young minds to stretch beyond the confines of predetermined narratives and reimagine the bounds of their future.

At the core of this vital process lies the intentional, comprehensive fostering of a strong sense of self in Black girls, thereby ensuring that they are aware of their history, their resilience, and their immense potential. This foundational identity extends beyond the superficial, transcending ephemeral trends and temporal labels to forge a connection with the indelible legacy of the generations that have gone before them. From the stories of triumph in the face of daunting adversity to the quiet, yet forceful deliberations of women who have steered the course of history, the narratives of our ancestors yield fertile ground for the cultivation of the next generation of Black leaders.

To achieve this, the thirst for knowledge must be instilled in young Black women at the earliest stages of their development, thus guiding them on the path of educational excellence and self-discovery. A comprehensive and inclusive curriculum—one that ensures a truthful and authentic representation of Black history—plays a crucial role in inculcating a strong self-image and self-identity. Consequently, a well-rounded education serves as the breeding ground for critical thinking, creative problem-solving, and a deep appreciation for the complexities and intersections of identity in their lives.

Moreover, the cultivation of empowerment in our future leaders is multifaceted, encompassing not only the encouragement and recognition of their individual strengths and talents but also the creation of spaces that champion and amplify Black girls' voices, perspectives, and ideas. Platforms such as community-led creative arts programs, mentoring initiatives, and civic engagement workshops equip young Black women with the tools and confidence they need to navigate the world and confront the challenges that they will undoubtedly face in their journey.

As we unlock the infinite potential inherent in the souls of these future leaders, it is our collective imperative to nurture and safeguard the freedom of self-expression for Black girls. In our hands, we hold the power to create an environment that allows these budding hearts to blossom—to sing their unique song, to dance with unbridled joy, and to write the stories that will change the course of history. It is through self-expression that our young girls develop the necessary self-appreciation and self-love that are the foundations for the immense wisdom needed to navigate life's many obstacles.

The seeds of resilience and eminence are already present within each and every young Black girl. Through the combined efforts of family, community, education, and mentorship, we have the unique power to create an environment that enables these seeds to thrive and grow. It is our responsibility to cultivate a space that nourishes these young minds and provides them with the sustenance they need to reach their full potential, much like the sun that casts its light upon the verdant landscape, imbuing life to the seeds that are waiting to blossom.

As these burgeoning leaders vie for spaces in the sun, asserting their claim to a brighter, richer future, we—who have been entrusted with the honor, privilege, and responsibility of nurturing these seeds—will bear witness to their unfolding transformation. It is a metamorphosis born from the forces of resilience, endurance, and love—a dance choreographed to the rhythms of the past and the melodies of the future. And as we foster this emancipation of spirit, we will rejoice in the incandescent brilliance of the legacies they create, shining forth as beacons of hope and change for the generations yet to follow.

Owning Our Strengths: Embracing the Unique Talents and Contributions of Black Women

In a world that often seeks to reduce the multiplicity of Black women's experiences to a single, monolithic narrative, it is essential to disrupt these restrictive constructs and embrace the unique talents, strengths, and contributions that Black women bring into various spaces. To own our strengths is to recognize and celebrate our distinct capabilities and achievements, acknowledging that we are not defined by the limitations that society seeks to impose upon us, but by the boundless expanses of our ingenuity, creativity, and resilience.

Throughout history, Black women have brought forth a dazzling array of skills and talents, demonstrating profound expertise in diverse fields. From the mesmerizing prose of Zora Neale Hurston to the larger-than-life oratory skills of Sojourner Truth, the captivating choreography of Alvin Ailey to the influential collages and mixed-media art of Betye Saar, the plethora of unique talents and contributions of Black women is testament to the depth and breadth of our potential and abilities. Despite myriad challenges and obstacles, Black women have persevered, excelling not only in the endeavors that they were allowed to pursue, but also in breaking the barriers that were forcibly placed before them.

Take, for instance, the story of Madame C.J. Walker, who defied societal restrictions to become the first self-made female millionaire in America. Born to formerly enslaved parents in the 1860s, Walker ventured into the world of entrepreneurship armed with unyielding determination and a desire to create opportunities for others. Through her ingenuity, she developed and marketed a line of hair care products explicitly designed for Black women, a previously untapped market. Over the course of her career, she employed and trained thousands of Black women as sales agents, and in doing so, built the foundation for the economic autonomy and agency for scores of Black women.

The same indomitable spirit that propelled Madame C.J. Walker to the heights of success can be seen in other transformative figures like Sister Rosetta Tharpe, the electric guitar pioneer who fundamentally shaped the course of modern music. Often referred to as the "Godmother of Rock and Roll," Tharpe disproved the stereotypes that sought to box Black women into specific roles and expectations. By merging her background in gospel music with the burgeoning sounds of rhythm and blues, she introduced an innovative new style that defied categorization, leaving an indelible mark on the landscape of American music.

In acknowledging and celebrating Black women's multifaceted talents and contributions, we also challenge the societal norms and expectations that continue to restrain and constrict us. For young Black girls growing up in the shadow of prescribed narratives, witnessing the vast range of Black women's accomplishments and endeavors is both empowering and transformative. It provides a tangible connection to their potential, fostering self-esteem and inspiring them to redefine the limits of their creativity and ambition. Essential to this process of affirming our strengths, is the cultivation of spaces - both physical and virtual - where Black women can share their work, stories, and experiences. This allows the collective narrative to be enriched, diversified, and preserved for future generations.

In today's interconnected world, the visibility and recognition of Black women's talents and contributions are gradually expanding. Social media platforms have allowed many to share their art, connect with like-minded individuals, and build supportive communities, fostering a newfound sense of agency in shaping the portrayal of Black women. However, it remains essential that traditional spaces – educational institutions, workplaces, and media – also work to challenge preconceived notions and assumptions, creating an environment where the talents and voices of Black women can be amplified, unapologetically and authentically.

The process of reclaiming our strengths and abilities is not without challenge, as it often requires confronting the biases that have been internalized over time. Yet, as we stride boldly into the future, embracing both our individual and collective power, we forge a new narrative – a narrative that defies the age-old constraints, celebrates the multifarious talents and contributions of Black women, and embraces the iridescent spectrum of our brilliance. This redefining of the narrative has the power to invigorate our connections to the past and craft a richer, more expansive legacy for the generations to come. As we bask in the brilliance of our ancestors and savor the splendor of their enduring strength, we stand on the precipice of a new epoch: an era where the boundless essence of Black women's talents and contributions are revered, celebrated, and cherished, thereby illuminating the indomitable spirit that has persevered through generations and the profound resilience that binds us all.

Passing the Torch: Empowering Young Black Women Through Mentorship and Support

As the inextinguishable embers of ancestral legacies pulse through veins and dance under the moonlit sky, there exists a sacred responsibility that extends beyond the mere responsibility of the self. This responsibility lies in the rhythms of the footsteps that echo softly amidst the rustling winds; it lies in the hush of the whispers that hold the secrets of generations yet to be born. This duty, entrusted to us— the keepers of ancient wisdom and timeless resilience—beckons us to undertake the noble endeavor of passing the torch to the young Black women who will one day ascend to their rightful place as leaders, visionaries, and pillars of strength.

Within the shadows that drape the contours of our history, there is a profound treasure trove of knowledge, insight, and inspiration that has been cultivated through the generations: stories wrought from iron, molded by the fires of adversity, and tempered by the icy streams of unwavering endurance. These stories contain within themselves the seeds of empowerment that, when sown into the fertile soil of young minds, will give rise to a verdant garden of possibility and potential. Nurtured carefully, with steady hands and unwavering resolve, these seeds will be given the sustenance they require to grow and flourish, spreading their roots and tendrils to create new spaces and worlds where Black women can rise and be seen in the full spectrum of their brilliance.

This process of transmission—of passing the torch from one generation to the next—begins with the bonding of mentors and mentees. It is through this relationship that the stories of the past are woven together with the dreams of the future, creating a tapestry that both honors the resilience of the past and inspires the growth of the future. Mentorship can take various forms; it may be rooted in the guidance and wisdom of older relatives, the nurturing and counsel of educators and skilled professionals, or the inspiring examples of trailblazers from various fields. Regardless of the form it takes, the intention remains the same: to offer support, foster growth, and nurture the self-confidence that arises from the realization of one's potential.

Powerful examples of trailblazing mentors who have paved the path for future generations of Black women are everywhere around us. Consider the indomitable Maya Angelou, who not only established a legacy of critical thought and poetic expression that continues to ripple through the hearts and minds of readers worldwide, but also offered her wisdom and guidance to those who sought the luminous brilliance of her words and soul. Driven by the undeniable truth that "we are each other's harvest; we are each other's business; we are each other's magnitude and bond," Angelou's approach to mentorship was grounded in a fundamental belief in the interconnectedness of all beings and the power of shared experience in lighting the way for future generations.

The value of mentorship as a potent force for empowerment can also be found within the ever-evolving realms of science, technology, engineering, and mathematics (STEM). Dr. Mae Jemison, a legend in her own right as the first Black woman in space, has long championed the cause of encouraging and supporting the education and interests of young Black women in these lesser-represented fields. Through her various initiatives, including The Earth We Share science camp, that engage students globally, Dr. Jemison has inspired thousands of young Black girls to carve a place for themselves and shatter the glass ceilings that stifle their boundless promise.

To cultivate and nourish the ascendance of these young Black women, it is essential that the environments in which they learn, grow, and thrive are innately nurturing and infused with the collective energy of love, affirmation, and trust. In these safe spaces, free from the predatory claws of violative gazes and oppressive narratives, young Black women can connect with mentors, forge bonds with their peers, and explore the depths of their potential without fear of judgment or derision. Moreover, these spaces are vital in fostering a sense of sisterhood and collaboration, dispelling the insidious belief that there is a finite supply of opportunities and resources that must be fought over. As this spirit of camaraderie and unity reigns supreme, the environments that nurture it shall only continue to grow in strength, as will the next generation of Black women leaders.

In conclusion, the act of passing the torch to young Black women offers a potent opportunity to reshape the broader narrative that encompasses the lives and experiences of Black women throughout history. By infusing the hearts and minds of the next generation with the incandescent brilliance of the mentors who have forged the path, we can nurture an environment that fosters growth, understanding, and, ultimately, transformation. Just as the sun, in its boundless wisdom, waits on the horizon each night, so too, shall we, the keepers of the legacies that have come before, bear witness to the emergence of the new day, shining forth with the luminosity of myriad stars— each one a testament to the boundless potential of mentorship.

Creating a New Narrative: The Importance of Storytelling and Sharing Personal Experiences

As the sun sets on a world forged by the indelible ink of past narratives, a new dawn breaks, illuminating the boundless possibilities that lie in the uncharted territories of the imagination. The empowering and transformative act of storytelling, long held as a sacred responsibility by our ancestors, has not waned in significance. Rather, it has evolved dramatically, encompassing not only the oral and written traditions of yore, but also the profusion of digital and social media formats that have come to define the contemporary zeitgeist.

The importance of storytelling within the experiences of Black women cannot be overstated, as it represents an intrinsic and enduring facet of our collective existence. Through the art of sharing stories and personal experiences, we weave the intricate tapestry of our history, seeking to breathe life into the voices silenced by time and to rekindle the fires that forged the legacies of those who came before us. Simultaneously, storytelling allows us to shatter the chains of imposed narrative restraints and to celebrate the multiplicity of individual voices, experiences, and perspectives that constitute the richly diverse fabric of our collective journey.

In embracing the power of storytelling, we bear witness to the profound resilience and strength that characterize the Black female experience. The tales of our ancestors – the stories wrought from their triumphs, sorrows, and unwavering determination – impart invaluable wisdom and guidance to those who follow in their footsteps. By sharing our stories, we offer solace to those navigating the treacherous waters of adversity, providing a beacon of hope in moments of despair and a balm to soothe the emotional wounds inflicted by the struggles inherent in one's journey.

Consider, for instance, the visceral impact of Maya Angelou's "I Know Why the Caged Bird Sings," a literary masterpiece that captures the essence of the liberating power of storytelling in the face of adversity. Through her writing, Angelou was able to transcend the constraints of societal expectations, creating an enduring legacy that continues to inspire and empower generations of Black women. Similarly, the story of Malorie Blackman, the first Black Children's Laureate, offers a narrative of triumph that defies the limitations bestowed upon her by a world that sought to deny her talent and potential. By penning the groundbreaking "Noughts & Crosses" series and providing a much-needed representation of Black characters within the realm of literature, she gave voice to the aspirations of countless young Black girls who had been invisible within the pages of the written word.

The potential for storytelling to dismantle harmful myths and empower women is not limited to the realm of written literature; it can also manifest in the digital sphere. Much like the ancient bards and griots, who preserved the oral traditions of their communities, contemporary Black women have harnessed the power of storytelling through platforms such as blogs, podcasting, and social media, amplifying their voices to shatter oppressive stereotypes and assert their agency. Take, for instance, the work of creators like Issa Rae, whose online web series "The Misadventures of Awkward Black Girl" gave life to the experiences of Black women in a manner that was both humorous and relatable, challenging the monolithic portrayals often seen in mainstream media.

In this new era of storytelling, Black women are reclaiming the narratives that have long defined them, molding and shaping them in their own image. This act of reclamation, facilitated by the myriad digital platforms at our disposal, allows us to chart a new and dynamic course, one that celebrates the full spectrum of our identities and experiences. This collective act of reclamation not only empowers the storytellers themselves, but it also fosters a sense of community and solidarity among those who partake in the stories, opening doors to meaningful discourse, authentic connections, and shared understanding.

As we journey into the uncharted realms of possibility and expression, it is essential that we do so with intention and purpose, mindful of the power that our words and stories hold. We must approach our role as storytellers with the solemn gravity that it warrants, endeavoring always to uplift, inspire, and bear witness to the multitude of voices that have long gone unheard. It is through our stories that we shall write the future, sowing seeds of empowerment and resilience for generations to come.

As this new narrative unfolds, the echoes of our ancestors' wisdom reverberate throughout the halls of history, reminding us of the unparalleled strength and tenacity that have always defined the Black female experience. In this world, where stories are spun like webs of infinite possibility and the voices of generations past merge with the whispers of the present, the power of storytelling nurtures our collective soul, beckoning us onwards, towards a future where we, the descendants of the indomitable empresses and unconquerable warrior queens, can ascend to our rightful place as the architects of a new and glorious epoch.

Building a Better Future: Harnessing the Power of Community and Collaboration to Shape the Legacy of Black Women

As we venture forth into the boundless landscape of possibility, seeking to build a better future that honors the triumphs and surmounts the tribulations of Black women throughout history, we must turn our gaze inward, exploring the recesses of our collective soul in pursuit of unity, solidarity, and empowerment. It is within these hallowed chambers that we find the key to the unprecedented transformation that lies within our grasp, a metamorphosis fueled by the inexhaustible strength of community and collaboration.

Recalling the struggles and resilience of our predecessors, it becomes evident that the advancement and liberation of Black women have always been predicated upon a foundation of shared experience, empathy, and mutual support. Consider, for example, the courage exhibited by Harriet Tubman, who, despite the suffocating tendrils of darkness that sought to encircle her within a life of bondage and enslavement, chose to make the arduous journey toward freedom not only for herself, but for countless others who dared to believe in a world unshackled from the chains of subjugation. As Tubman forged the path of the Underground Railroad, impelled by the steadfast belief that "every great dream begins with a dreamer," she exemplified the power of community and collaboration in shaping a new narrative that extolled the virtues of courage, resilience, and defiance.

Similar examples abound in other spheres of Black women's influence, from the pioneering activism of Ida B. Wells, whose unyielding dedication to the pursuit of social justice through her work as a journalist and suffragist, to the incandescent brilliance of Toni Morrison, whose writing illuminated the manifold intricacies of the Black female experience, ultimately carving a space within the annals of literary history for voices that had long been silenced. Throughout these narratives, a common thread emerges: the power of community and collaboration to create lasting change, inspiring future generations and challenging the status quo.

In order to harness the transformative force of community and collaboration, we must first actively confront and dismantle the insidious barriers that hinder our collective progress, such as internalized racism, colorism, and competition for limited resources and opportunities. By creating spaces that promote honest dialogue, self-reflection, and educational enlightenment, we can foster a culture of healing, growth, and sisterhood, bound together by a shared dedication to the pursuit of a brighter future for all.

Moreover, as we cultivate an environment rooted in collaboration, it is essential that we remain mindful of the importance of representation and inclusivity within our collective efforts. By actively seeking out diverse perspectives and experiences, we can create a rich and multifaceted mosaic that honors the vast array of backgrounds and identities that comprise the Black female experience. In doing so, we ensure that our journey toward empowerment is both grounded in authenticity and fueled by a commitment to intersectional equity.

The power of community and collaboration is further underscored by the emergence of grassroots organizations and movements that champion the causes and needs of Black women globally. These initiatives, spearheaded by visionary leaders who recognize the paramount importance of collective action, serve as powerful reminders of the indomitable strength and resilience that abound when we join forces in pursuit of a common goal. Through these collaborative efforts, we are not only able to effect tangible change within our communities, but we also contribute to the broader reclamation of agency and autonomy for Black women worldwide.

As we stand now at the precipice of an unparalleled era of transformation and growth, it is our sacred duty to embrace the power of community and collaboration to shape the legacy of Black women. In unison, we must weave threads of healing, empowerment, and unity into the tapestry of our collective narrative, boldly entwining the past and the present to create a future that reverberates with the echoes of inextinguishable strength, resilience, and boundless possibility.

As we look toward the dawn of a new day, emerging with the promise of a brighter future. In this liminal space betwixt night and day, we gather our strength, our wisdom, and our courage, purposefully striding forth as a unified force, shaped by the collective power of community and collaboration—and imbued with the unyielding spirit that has, and shall always, define Black women.

THE EMPOWERED ROOTS MOVEMENT: REDEFINING THE NARRATIVE OF BLACK WOMEN

As we delve into the Empowered Roots Movement, we stand witness to a remarkable paradigm shift, a collective awakening that transcends the boundaries of what we thought possible and redefines the narrative of Black women. This movement, fueled by passion and resilience, harnesses the vast potential within us, seeking not only to dismantle existing oppressive structures but also to reshape our perceptions and create a new world where our identity and agency are celebrated and valued.

The Empowered Roots Movement finds its origin in the countless moments of resistance, strength, and triumph that have defined the Black female experience. It is the culmination of the unwavering spirit of our ancestors, who birthed revolutions, pioneered social justice movements, and refused to be silenced in the face of adversity. As we carry forth their indomitable spirit, we are guided by the knowledge that the stories we tell about ourselves have the power to shape our futures, both individually and collectively.

One of the most crucial aspects of the Empowered Roots Movement is the disruption and dismantling of stereotypes that have long plagued Black women. For far too long, our identities have been misrepresented and diminished, confined within the constraints of unfounded myths that have sought to undermine our strength, intellect, and autonomy. The Empowered Roots Movement challenges these harmful narratives head-on, seeking to reclaim our identity and showcase the diverse, multifaceted aspects of our lives. Through the careful examination and redefinition of long-held beliefs, we are gradually breaking free from the fetters of inequality and asserting our rightful place as leaders, change-makers, and visionaries.

At the forefront of the Empowered Roots Movement are trailblazing women who embody the essence of renaissance and resurgence. Eschewing the limitations imposed upon them, these leaders have dared to step into their power and use their platforms to ignite change. From Ava DuVernay, who continually breaks boundaries and subverts expectations with her groundbreaking films and television shows, to Chimamanda Ngozi Adichie, whose literary prowess and insightful commentary have captivated audiences across the globe, these women serve as living embodiments of the transformative potential that lies within us all. Their collective efforts demonstrate the undeniable power and resilience of Black women, inspiring countless others to rise above adversity and redefine their stories on their own terms.

The undeniable impact of social media on the Empowered Roots Movement cannot be ignored. These technological platforms have reconfigured the landscape of storytelling and connection, enabling Black women to amplify their voices and share their experiences with a global audience. Social media has provided us with an unparalleled opportunity to challenge misconstrued narratives and celebrate our diversity, forging new connections based on shared understanding, authenticity, and support. In utilizing these tools, we harness the collective strength of our community to catalyze change from within.

Integral to the ethos of the Empowered Roots Movement is the imperative to empower the next generation of Black women. Through ongoing efforts to provide education, mentorship, and support, we are not only investing in the future of our community but also ensuring that the torch of resilience and determination is passed on to those who will carry our legacy forward. By instilling in them the knowledge of their worth, their capabilities, and their potential, we are fostering an environment wherein they are poised to break barriers, defy expectations, and reshape the course of history.

The movement also demands the re-evaluation and transformation of institutional systems that have long perpetuated harmful narratives and restricted opportunities for Black women. By advocating for comprehensive change within educational systems, media representation, and frameworks of power, we are working towards dismantling oppressive structures that hinder progress. This commitment to pushing for systemic change serves as a testament to the unyielding spirit of the Empowered Roots Movement and its potential to create lasting, meaningful change.

A crucial aspect of the Empowered Roots Movement is the incorporation of intersectionality, acknowledging the ways race, gender, sexuality, and other social factors converge to impact the experiences of Black women. By recognizing these intersections and striving to broaden inclusivity, the movement fosters a sense of belonging, allowing all Black women to see themselves reflected within the tapestry of our shared legacy of resilience.

As we continue our journey within the Empowered Roots Movement, it is essential that we remain steadfast in our dedication to redefining the narrative of Black women, boldly challenging the status quo and claiming our rightful place in the forefront of the struggle for equity and justice. Our collective efforts within this movement are not simply acts of defiance or resistance; they are acts of reclamation, of re-writing our stories, and of envisioning a future where our voices ring loud and clear, echoing the indomitable spirit that has long defined our existence.

As we stand on the precipice of transformative change, our eyes fixed on a horizon illuminated by the promise of a brighter day, let us remain ever-vigilant in our pursuit of a new world, where the echo of our ancestors' indomitable resilience resonates through the halls of history, and the Empowered Roots Movement serves as a testament to the limitless potential within Black women's indelible spirit.

The Movement Redefined: A New Chapter Begins

The Empowered Roots Movement on its surface may seem like a rising wave of black women claiming their rightful space in the world. Yet, it goes far deeper than that; it transcends mere surface-level activism and breaks the shackles of time itself. It rises like a phoenix from the ashes of the past, carrying on the indomitable spirit of generations of black women who have fought for their rights and recognition. This is a movement that begins with a seed planted in the heart of history and grows in tandem with each life touched by its fruition, transforming not just the narrative of today but laying the groundwork for the tapestry of the future.

To truly behold the magnitude of this paradigm shift, we must first examine our history. We must look back upon the faces and voices of generations past—of our great-grandmothers and the grandmothers before them—and listen to the stories they shared. These narratives are whispers in time, echoes of resilience and strength that have inspired countless generations to rise against adversity. They remind us of the unbroken chain connecting us to our ancestors, a tether that transcends the boundaries of age and experience.

As we bear witness to the extraordinary tapestry that is the Empowered Roots Movement, we come to realize that its very foundation is built upon a rich legacy of determination and defiance. This movement is simultaneously ancient and burgeoning, an acknowledgement of the transcendental power within every black woman to overcome and thrive in spite of systemic barriers. It is a movement that refuses to be constrained by the limitations of the past and embraces the bold unknown of the evolving story, diving headfirst into a narrative that is rapidly being redefined.

Central to the Empowered Roots Movement is the recognition that the power to reshape our futures lies within the strength of our collective voices. Bold and unyielding, the women at the forefront of this movement embody the essence of transformation and defiance, refusing to be pigeonholed or dismissed. They challenge the norms that have long shaped the narratives around black womanhood and unabashedly demand that a new narrative emerges—one that not only embraces the diversity of black women but also shatters the mold, disrupting the status quo by creating space for the expression of our true selves.

Within this extraordinary paradigm shift, we find ourselves as participants and agents of change. We look back to our ancestors with gratitude for their unwavering resolve and draw from their wisdom as we charge forth into new territory. Yet, we also forge ahead with fearless determination as we step into our roles as architects of the future, recognizing that our voices can birth a new reality—one that no longer adheres to the limitations of the past.

The progression of the Empowered Roots Movement is rapid and unrelenting, a swift tide that becomes stronger with each new voice that rises against the currents of traditional thought and structural barriers. It is informed by a depth of knowledge and understanding, as well as an unwavering conviction in the ability of black women to rise above the limitations imposed by societal constructs.

As we embark on this journey into uncharted territory, we are guided by the knowledge that our steps are not mere footprints in the sand; we are the pathfinders, the cartographers of an entirely new dimension, laying the groundwork for a future that we may not yet know the full extent of. And while the road ahead may sometimes appear uncertain and the challenges formidable, the Empowered Roots Movement reminds us that we are not alone. It provides us with the tools and the knowledge to forge ahead with confidence and self-belief, reassured by the knowledge that in our hearts and minds lies a wealth of ancestral wisdom and an indomitable spirit that cannot be extinguished.

The birth of the Empowered Roots Movement is not simply a call for change; it is a metamorphosis, a revolution, and the dawning of a new era. It is the awakening of a collective consciousness that refuses to be silenced, one that roars with the mighty power of a thousand voices united in purpose and destiny. This is more than just a movement; it is a revival of a heritage and energy that pulses through the veins of black women across generations, an energy that courses through the very fabric of space and time, summoning us to rise and reshape our stories and our destiny at long last.

Breaking the Mold: New Perspectives on Black Womanhood

The journey to disrupt stereotypes and change perceptions of Black women is a complex, multifaceted undertaking that requires courage, resilience, and the unwavering belief in the transformative power of truth. As we traverse the landscape of our collective narrative, we are often confronted with deeply entrenched myths and clichés, the residue of centuries-long indoctrination into a limiting and often degrading discourse. Yet it is precisely by charting these unfamiliar territories that we come to understand the scope of our potential and the richness of our shared experience.

One of the most insidious stereotypes embedded in the fabric of Black women's lives is the myth of the "angry Black woman." This caricature, perpetuated throughout history, seeks to delegitimize the authentic emotions and experiences of Black women by casting them as unreasonably aggressive and irritable. To dismantle this stereotype, it is vital that we first understand its roots and the ways in which it has been weaponized to invalidate and silence the voices of Black women. This understanding allows us to interrogate and ultimately subvert the power dynamics that underpin this myth, reclaiming our right to fully express our emotions without fear of being summarily dismissed.

As we strive to dismantle the myth of the "angry Black woman," we are also confronted with an equally pernicious stereotype: the "strong Black woman." This narrative, which appears on the surface to be a compliment, is equally limiting and dehumanizing in its insistence that Black women are impervious to pain and suffering. This stereotype effaces the vulnerability and tenderness inherent in the human experience and robs Black women of the space to express their many dimensions, from joy to despair, and everything in between. By challenging the narrative of the "strong Black woman," we expose the underlying assumptions about the limitations upon our emotional repertoire and begin to dismantle the structures that uphold this myth.

Another powerful means of disrupting stereotypes is through storytelling. By reclaiming our narratives and shedding light on the vast spectrum of Black women's lives, we challenge preconceived notions about our capabilities, desires, and dreams. Through stories, we excavate the buried truths of our ancestors, preserving and honoring their voices, as well as breathing new life into their legacies. We bear witness to the evolution of our community, from its roots in antiquity to its present and future manifestations.

In this quest for authenticity, we must look to the women who have come before us, as well as those who walk beside us, and ask ourselves how our own experiences might challenge the dominant narrative. We must ask ourselves how the unspoken stories of our sisters might disrupt the stereotypes that have been imposed upon us. These are the pivotal moments of rupture and revelation, the moments when the faint glimmers of a new narrative begin to emerge, and the foundation upon which we will build our future.

There are countless examples of Black women who have defied the stereotypes and forged their paths, breaking through barriers and refusing to be confined by the expectations that society has placed upon them. From Michelle Obama, a powerful advocate for education and health, transcending the role of the traditional First Lady, to Serena Williams, transcending barriers in sport, business, and philanthropy, these women serve as inspiring reminders of the potency of resilience and the transformative potential of determination.

By centering the experiences of Black women and amplifying their voices in the media, arts, and social justice movements, we begin to dismantle the monolithic representations that have long plagued our community. We witness the emergence of a new narrative, one that celebrates the multiplicity and richness of Black women's experiences, highlights their strength and wisdom, and acknowledges their vulnerability and humanity.

In closing, the process of disrupting stereotypes and changing perceptions of Black women is a gradual and complex undertaking. However, as we continue to unearth the buried truths of our ancestors, to amplify the voices of those who have been silenced, and to reclaim our narrative, we sew the seeds of a revolution that promises to transform not only our own lives but the lives of generations to come. A revolution that recognizes the true potential of Black women, honoring their complexity and resilience, and painting a vivid, authentic picture of who we are and what we can become.

Leading Lights: Profiles in Courage and Innovation

Captivating figures who brim with vim and spirit have shaped the contours of our collective memory, becoming wayfinders for the manifold generations that followed. The Empowered Roots Movement is no exception – forged in the crucible of determination and defiance, the women driving this movement show a powerful versatility of leadership that transcends age, geography, and vocation. Within their diverse experiences, we glimpse the essence of radical change, the profound breaking away from archaic narratives and the daring push toward a future where the potential of black women remains no longer a dormant seed buried deep within the soil, but a glorious blossoming tree.

One such leader is Tarana Burke, a civil rights activist and founder of the "Me Too" movement. Her work has long advocated for the most marginalized communities, from providing safe spaces for survivors of sexual violence to creating a support network for young women of color. Her work profoundly transforms the conversation around sexual assault, centering it on empathy, solidarity, and resilience. Tarana's role in challenging the status quo culminates in the creation of a new narrative, one that not only empowers survivors to come forward but also generates a global call to action.

Equally compelling is the story of Patrisse Cullors, a powerhouse artist, organizer, and co-founder of the Black Lives Matter movement. Channeling her passion for justice and equality, she has been instrumental in cultivating a robust vision for the future, wherein black lives hold an intrinsic value that is not debatable or conditional. Her work transcends the realm of activism, recognizing the indispensability of holistic solutions that tackle the myriad facets of systemic inequality: from mental health and education to criminal justice reform. Patrisse's trajectory is a testament to the indomitable power of courage and resolve, as she casts a blazing light on the unconquerable spirit that propels the Empowered Roots Movement.

Similarly, the literary sphere holds a treasure trove of transformative figures such as Chimamanda Ngozi Adichie, the celebrated Nigerian author, feminist, and thought leader. Her works, rooted in the richness of African culture and history, bestow upon black women a nuanced and multilayered representation that defies unidimensional narratives. Chimamanda's undeniable ability to weave tales of truth, vulnerability, and strength paves the way for a new generation of storytellers – each imbued with the desire to combat erasure and amplify the plethora of experiences that shape black womanhood.

In the world of sport, we find the indomitable Serena Williams, a trailblazing tennis champion who defied the odds and shattered the barriers of an elitist white-dominated sport. As a black woman, Serena has faced criticism and discrimination throughout her career, and yet her power, grace, and unwavering dedication to her craft has led her to become one of the most revered athletes of all time. Serena's legacy inspires countless young girls to seize their dreams with unapologetic boldness and embrace the full breadth of their potential, undaunted by societal limitations.

A striking example in the political arena is the resolute Stacey Abrams, a former member of the Georgia State House, who has dedicated herself to the fight for voting rights, following her narrow defeat for the governorship of Georgia in a highly contested election marred by voter suppression. Unyielding in her fight for the right to vote, Stacey founded Fair Fight Action, an organization that tirelessly works to protect democracy, ensuring that every American has a voice in shaping the nation's future. Stacey Abrams' tenacious spirit encapsulates the essence of the Empowered Roots Movement, as she confidently contends with the structural barriers that seek to stifle black women's advancement and leadership.

It is amidst the diverse symphony of these remarkable voices that we locate a deeply profound sense of purpose that ties all these trailblazers together: the understanding that the uplifting and empowering of black women is an endeavor that reverberates across all realms, suffusing society with the endless possibilities that unfold when the shackles of restriction are undone. As we marvel at the leaders within the Empowered Roots Movement, we are invigorated with the belief that the seeds of change have been planted and that they will grow in strength and magnitude, ushering in an era of transformation that shall ripple across generations and remain indelible in our collective memory.

Digital Diaspora: Social Media Shaping Our Stories

The Empowered Roots Movement, a swelling collective of Black women calling for authentic representation and an end to oppressive stereotypes, is unequivocally indebted to the pervasive influence of social media. As a dynamic platform for grassroots activism, social media provides an unprecedented opportunity for Black women to reshape the discourse surrounding their experiences and forge connections across the vast diaspora. This digitized realm has contributed to the emergence of a powerful online community capable of challenging deeply entrenched narratives and catalyzing transformative change.

The most salient characteristic of social media's impact on the Empowered Roots Movement is its ability to amplify marginalized voices with often overlooked perspectives. Through creating and sharing content ranging from thought-provoking essays and incisive critique to heart-rendering poetry, Black women have harnessed the connective power of the internet to challenge hegemonic viewpoints and uplift one another in defiance of traditional media gatekeepers. Blogging platforms such as Medium and Tumblr, as well as multimedia sharing sites like Instagram and YouTube, allow Black women to take control of their narrative and vision for the future.

A striking example of this phenomenon is the rapid dissemination of thought pieces authored by Black women within the Twittersphere. Under the auspices of hashtags like #BlackGirlMagic and #SayHerName, these poignant analyses not only crystallize the unique struggles and triumphs of Black womanhood but also serve as a clarion call for intersectional solidarity. In this sense, social media serves as a conduit for the proliferation of counter-narratives that challenge preconceived notions and foster a more nuanced understanding of Black women's realities.

Moreover, the rise of social media influencers and personalities has played a crucial role in the popularization of the Empowered Roots

Movement. Black women entrepreneurs, artists, and activists utilize their digital reach to foster dialogue, support, and action around issues crucial to the upliftment of their community. These trailblazers, distinguished by their candor, boldness, and fierce commitment to social transformation, act as indispensable agents of change, steadily dismantling barriers that hinder the progress of Black women.

Furthermore, digital activism has engendered a groundswell of collective action that extends far beyond the confines of cyberspace. Social media has served as a potent vehicle for the organization and mobilization of protests, workshops, conferences, and other consciousness-raising events, which have catalyzed tangible change in societal attitudes and policies. The real-world impact of this digital network is perhaps most aptly illustrated by the meteoric rise of the Black Lives Matter movement, which can be traced back to its inception as a humble hashtag on Twitter.

The internet, despite its potential as an emancipatory force, is not without its pitfalls. The prevalence of cyberbullying, doxxing, and targeted harassment against prominent Black women highlights the persistence of racial and gendered violence in the digital sphere. Nevertheless, these setbacks only serve to underscore the importance of cultivating safe online spaces where Black women can connect, communicate, and commiserate without fear of retribution or reprisal.

As we bear witness to the burgeoning vitality of the Empowered Roots Movement, it becomes impossible to overlook the unmistakable imprint of social media on its development. Indeed, social media has proven to be a formidable engine propelling the Movement forward, providing the necessary fuel for radical exploration and collaboration. Amidst the ever-evolving tapestry of the digital landscape, we glimpse a future where the stories, aspirations, and dreams of Black women are no longer relegated to the shadows but embraced in the warm embrace of recognition, admiration, and profound respect. This, in turn, begets a world where the boundless possibilities of Black women's potential glow like constellations, illuminating the path toward a resplendent future, carved out by the unyielding determination and unwavering spirit that define the Empowered Roots Movement.

Tomorrow's Trailblazers: Nurturing Young Black Minds

For millennia, young Black girls have been entrusted with the weight of a remarkable legacy: one that teems with the memories of compelling heroines who have woven a tapestry of resilience and innovation through the annals of history. This vibrant endowment is not bestowed lightly, for it is through the nurturance and upliftment of these nascent spirits that the Empowered Roots Movement finds its sustenance, its lifeblood, and its indomitable heart. As we cast our gaze upon the landscape of their potential, we are invariably called to action, spurred by the belief that young Black girls possess an uncanny alchehest of possibilities, awaiting only the unwavering support and guidance of those who dare to invest in their worth.

Critical to any effort to empower young Black girls is the work of dismantling narratives that hinge their value upon limiting social constructs. This begins, inarguably, at the level of education, where young minds are propelled to question the received wisdom that governs their lives. Creating pedagogies that integrate the boundless achievements of Black women from diverse fields, cultures, and periods in history are revolutionary acts, for they foster pride, inspiration, and a profound sense of belonging in the face of a world that oftentimes renders young Black girls invisible. Through this experiential lens, they can glimpse the array of futures that stretch forth, beckoning them with the promise of change and radiant self-discovery.

Equally imperative is the nurturing of spaces where the creativity and emotional intelligence of young Black girls can flourish. The world of artistic expression, from visual arts and theater to literature and dance, holds a wealth of transformative potential, enabling youth to transmute their complex experiences and emotions into a stunning tableau of singular truth, passion, and exuberance. By fostering environments that cherish their creative energy, we offer young Black girls the opportunity to forge their own pathways of healing and self-expression, transcending the boundaries set by a society that seeks to silence their authentic voices.

Yet this endeavor to interrogate and restructure the world around them would be rendered incomplete without the cultivation of a staunch and unbreakable faith in their own innate capacities. Empowering young Black girls necessitates imbuing them with a sense of unassailable self-esteem, one that draws from the deep wellspring of love bestowed upon them by their communities, families, and mentors. This fortitude of spirit is a powerful antidote to the trials they will inevitably face, granting them the resilience and emotional wherewithal to navigate life with audacity and grace.

The power of mentorship, too, cannot be underestimated in this critical quest. Identifying and promoting strong role models who embody the values and ideals of the Empowered Roots Movement has the potential to instill confidence, determination, and hope in the hearts of young Black girls. Being able to witness first-hand the triumphs and challenges faced by dynamic figures from diverse walks of life imparts priceless wisdom, effectively bridging the gulf between generations and enabling a seamless transmission of knowledge, experience, and empowering strategies.

Finally, it is essential to remember that the empowerment of young Black girls is not a solitary task, but rather a collective endeavor that demands a communal spirit of solidarity and collaboration. The movement must weave an intricate web of support, encompassing all facets of society - from schools and community organizations to families and media outlets - in order to foster a holistic and sustainable model of growth, one that is inextricably grounded in the deep roots of love, wisdom, and fearless tenacity.

Thus, it is within the constellation of these principles that the movement for empowering young Black girls gains its momentum, unfurling a new paradigm of limitless potential and indomitable spirit.

As the torchbearers of this incandescent cause, we hold in our hands not only the opportunity but the responsibility to enrich and embolden the next generation - one that shall, in turn, pass the flame forward, illuminating a resplendent cosmos of a world shaped by their unabashed brilliance and courage. And in this radiant constellation, we behold glimpses of a powerful metamorphosis, a transcendent evolution, and a transcendent legacy that shall endure for generations to come.

Changing the Game: Education and Media's Role in Transformation

It is within the hallowed walls of educational institutions and through the vast channels of media that the narrative of Black women, so often confined by the shackles of stereotype and misrepresentation, finds the fertile ground to bloom into a rich tapestry of identity, complexity, and empowerment. Intrinsically interwoven into the fabric of the Empowered Roots Movement, these two formidable pillars of society possess the remarkable capacity to reshape both perceptions and realities for Black women, carving out a brave new world where the myriad hues of their stories are afforded the dignity and prominence they so richly deserve.

In examining the role of education as a catalyst for change, we inevitably encounter the concept of critical pedagogy, an emancipatory approach to education that calls forth the radical act of questioning, deconstructing, and, ultimately, transforming the structures and narratives that govern our lives. Envisioned as a crucible of empowerment, critical pedagogy asks Black women to break free from the shackles of passive acceptance, embracing instead the dynamic spirit of inquiry, and engaging in a relentless quest for knowledge and self-realization. By interrogating the status quo, Black women pave the way for the emergence of alternative discourses and paradigms, which in turn contribute to the broader tapestry of the Empowered Roots Movement.

This intellectual spirit of exploration is nourished by revised curricula and pedagogical approaches that weave a rich and intricate harmony of diverse voices, perspectives, and histories into the fabric of education. By shifting focus from Eurocentric narratives, educational institutions provide a more inclusive and representative account of our shared human experience, embracing the vibrant legacy of Black women leaders, thinkers, and creators who have shaped the contours of history. The incorporation of this diverse tapestry of wisdom transcends mere tokenism by fostering a profound sense of pride, connection, and aspiration among Black women, galvanized by the knowledge of their forebearers' resilience and triumphs.

Parallel to the transformative power of education, the expansive realm of media holds a unique sway over the hearts and minds of society, offering fertile ground for the redefinition of narratives surrounding Black women. The emergence of trailblazing creatives, from visionary filmmakers like Ava DuVernay, to groundbreaking television creators such as Shonda Rhimes and Issa Rae, signals a seismic shift in the portrayal of Black women on screen, capturing their multifaceted humanity with authenticity and nuance. These intrepid storytellers construct a cinematic landscape brimming with the complexity and depth of Black women's experiences, dismantling longstanding tropes and stereotypes by nurturing an environment that celebrates the diverse spectrum of Black womanhood.

Moreover, the changing media landscape - characterized by the rise of social media platforms, streaming services, and digital journalism - begins to shatter the traditional stronghold of gatekeepers, affording Black women an unprecedented opportunity to claim agency over their narratives. Whether through powerful visual images or searing, insightful prose, Black women step boldly into a world where their perspectives, no longer silenced or sidelined, mold and shape the contours of societal discourse. In this brave new arena of possibility, they find themselves equipped with the technology and tools to not only participate in, but to lead the conversation.

As the realm of education and media continues to morph and adapt, it becomes clear that the true power of institutional change resides in those who dare to envision a world beyond the constraints of convention, who refuse to be shackled by the narratives imposed upon them. By ardently pursuing the democratization of knowledge and striving for representation in every facet of society, those who comprise the Empowered Roots Movement propel the world toward a future that is resplendent with the vibrant colors of diversity, a tableau that is a testament to the richness of the human experience.

Unity in Diversity: Expanding the Circle of Inclusion

As we stand at the dawn of a new era, the Empowered Roots Movement is poised to usher in an unprecedented wave of change. Guided by the spirit of our ancestors, the Movement harnesses the unwavering resilience, wisdom, and fortitude of Black women to forge a world that transcends the limitations imposed by conventional narratives. At the heart of this understanding is the concept of intersectionality - a crucial lens through which we can discern the intricate tapestry of identities, experiences, and power dynamics that shape the lives of Black women.

Coined by scholar and civil rights advocate Kimberlé Crenshaw, intersectionality emerged as a groundbreaking theoretical framework, urging us to examine the convergence of distinct social categories such as race, gender, and class, within the context of oppressive systems. Rather than viewing these facets of identity as isolated phenomena, intersectionality emphasizes the importance of considering the totality of their impact, shedding light on the unique struggles and triumphs faced by Black women at the crossroads of multiple worlds. Indeed, this revolutionary framework offers both a critical understanding of the complex dynamics at play and a potent tool for forging a more inclusive and empowering future.

A striking illustration of the power of intersectionality lies in the remarkable life of the indomitable American poet Audre Lorde. Born to Caribbean immigrants, Lorde channeled her experiences as a Black, lesbian, feminist, and activist into her writing, crafting searing portraits of the myriad ways in which race, gender, sexuality, and class intersected within her life. As Lorde famously declared, "There is no such thing as a single-issue struggle because we do not live single issue lives." This timeless insight captures the essence of the Movement's commitment to intersectionality, encompassing the boundless diversity of Black women's lives.

Yet, the true transformative potential of intersectionality lies not only in the analysis of interlocking oppressions but also in its capacity to illuminate the paths towards inclusivity and solidarity. Embracing the rich tapestry of identities and experiences that comprise the Empowered Roots Movement necessitates dismantling the silos that have historically divided various struggles, erecting bridges of understanding across seemingly disparate worlds. In this act of unification, the Movement forges a potent force, capable of toppling long-standing barriers and effecting deep-rooted change.

For instance, the Movement actively seeks to create spaces that center the voices and experiences of Black women with disabilities, illuminating not only the systemic challenges they face but also the innumerable ways in which their presence and leadership enrich the collective cause. By uplifting these often-marginalized narratives, the Movement strengthens the bonds of sisterhood and paves the way for a more inclusive and holistic vision of empowerment.

Likewise, the vital importance of incorporating the transgender community and nonbinary individuals within the Movement's ambit cannot be overstated. As they continue to grapple with discrimination and erasure, the inclusion of transgender and nonbinary Black individuals adds a vital dimension to the struggle for collective liberation, magnifying its potential impact and deepening its resonance across the spectrum of human experiences.

As we stride forward, guided by the luminous legacy of our ancestors and emboldened by the flame of audacity that burns within our hearts, we recognize that the future belongs to those who dare to envision a world of unwavering solidarity and limitless potential. It is through this fervent commitment to intersectionality and inclusivity that the Empowered Roots Movement shall take root and flourish, heralding the dawn of a vibrant and transformative epoch, one that shall resonate with the echoes of our ancestors' dreams and the whispers of a future that is finally, truly, ours.

Looking Forward: The Evolution of Our Movement

In envisioning the future of the Empowered Roots Movement, we must recognize that the seeds of change have already been planted. In recent years, we have borne witness to an exhilarating wave of Black women claiming their rightful place at the table, from the meteoric rise of trailblazing political leaders like Stacey Abrams and Ilhan Omar, to the meteoric ascent of young voices battling for climate justice like Vanessa Nakate. In each of these unstoppable women, we see the spark of inspiration that promises to light the path for generations to come, fanning the flames of dreams that were once thought too audacious to be realized.

The future of the Empowered Roots Movement must rise to embrace this spirit of boundless possibility, nurturing a culture of support and collaboration that enables Black women from all walks of life to transcend the constraints of their circumstances and ascend to the summits of their fields. This entails the creation of targeted mentoring networks, scholarship programs, and capacity-building initiatives that harness the wisdom and resources of established Black women leaders, weaving a rich tapestry of mentorship and encouragement that will envelop young women and girls in a warm embrace of empowerment.

Moreover, the Movement will look beyond the shores of the United States, recognizing that the ties that bind Black women together span oceans and continents. In embracing a global outlook, the Empowered Roots Movement can forge powerful alliances with diasporic communities and grassroots organizations across the African continent and Caribbean archipelago, nurturing a vibrant exchange of ideas, strategies, and resources. The resulting cross-pollination of experiences, cultures, and wisdom will foster a truly dynamic global community of Black women, united in their quest for a brighter, more equitable future.

Casting our gaze towards the horizon, we foresee the Empowered Roots Movement diligently harnessing the potential of cutting-edge technology and social platforms to impact change across sectors. By equipping Black women with the tools to chart their own course in the rapidly evolving landscape of the digital age, the Movement will tap into an untapped wellspring of creativity, innovation, and leadership. Leveraging new media, artificial intelligence, and virtual reality, Black women will create immersive experiences that challenge the status quo, reach new audiences, and shatter glass ceilings, even beyond the realms of physical space.

In the realm of narrative and representation, we anticipate that the Empowered Roots Movement will continue to push the boundaries of genres, platforms, and mediums, compelling the world to confront their biases and create space for Black women to take the stage and showcase their limitless versatility. New narratives penned by the incisive pens of Black women will encompass not only the realism of their lives but also the boundless potential of speculative fiction, reimagining the foundations of society and probing the outer limits of the human experience. The collective imagination of the Movement, once unleashed, shall bear witness to a cultural renaissance, one that both honors and transcends the legacies of the past.

As we collectively lean into the uncharted territories of the future, our gaze rests not solely upon the lofty heights we wish to attain, but also upon the firmaments of sisterhood and solidarity upon which our aspirations must be grounded. The beating heart of the Empowered Roots Movement is the understanding that to reshape the world, we must first forge deep roots of kinship that can weather the storms of adversity; we must erect bridges of empathy that span chasms of difference, allowing us to journey hand in hand towards the horizon.

As Octavia Butler, the visionary writer, once proclaimed, "There is no end to what a living world will demand of you." Indeed, the future of the Empowered Roots Movement is an unwritten symphony to be composed from the beautiful cacophony of countless voices, a story that unfurls in real-time at the hands of each person who dares to wield their humanity as a force for change. In this future, we dare to believe that together, we can shape a world in which the legacies of our ancestors and the dreams of our descendants intertwine, forming a shimmering tapestry of hope that spans the vast expanse of time and space. In this future, the triumphs of the Empowered Roots Movement echo as a resounding chorus that reverberates through history, leaving Black women free to unfurl their wings and take flight.

A CELEBRATION OF US: HONORING THE JOURNEY OF BLACK WOMEN

As we embark on this critical juncture in history, it is of the utmost importance to pause and reflect - not only on the countless struggles and hardships faced by Black women throughout the ages, but also on their boundless resilience, determination, and triumphs. With a legacy rooted in the rich and diverse tapestry of our ancestral matriarchs, we must not simply acknowledge their perseverance in the face of adversity, but also celebrate and honor the immense potential and power they carried within their spirits, a power that remains alive and burning within the hearts of their descendants today.

The honoring and celebration of our journey must be centered around the inexhaustible potential of Black women and their descendants, who continue to build upon the foundation laid by those who came before them. The transcendent and transformative nature of this potential lies not just in our capacity to excel within our individual spheres, but in our ability to uplift and empower entire communities with our leadership, wisdom, and unwavering dedication to collective growth.

An excellent example of this intrinsic potential can be found within the realm of education, where Black women have made tremendous strides in overcoming systemic barriers and achieving groundbreaking accomplishments. Consider the inimitable Dr. Mae Jemison, the first Black woman to travel to space - an outstanding feat that serves as a powerful reminder of the limitless heights to which we can soar when we vigorously pursue our dreams and embrace our innate potentials. Dr. Jemison's story reverberates across generations, inspiring young Black girls to reach for the cosmos and shatter the glass ceiling of a predominantly white and male-dominated field.

In this spirit of embracing potential, we must also recognize the indispensable contributions of Black women as agents of change and pioneers in numerous fields, from politics and activism to science and technology. Visionaries like Congresswoman Shirley Chisholm, the first Black woman elected to the United States Congress, trailblazed paths that countless others have since followed. Her oft-repeated mantra, "If they don't give you a seat at the table, bring a folding chair," encapsulates the tenacity and resolve with which Black women have long confronted systemic barriers and demanded a place in the halls of power.

Furthermore, embracing potential necessitates acknowledging and harnessing the creative brilliance that has historically bloomed within Black women. The resplendent tapestry of literary, cinematic, and artistic works crafted by the likes of Toni Morrison, Julie Dash, and Kara Walker showcase the boundless capacity of Black women's creativity to challenge conventional narratives, produce evocative images, and spin yarns of transcendent beauty and depth. Inherent in these artistic accomplishments is the ability to redefine the contours of our shared reality, constructing new worlds and possibilities in which Black women and their descendants can fully inhabit and embrace their innate potential.

But to lift the veil on this immense potential is not simply to marvel at it in awe, but to pledge ourselves to the active cultivation and nurturing of its growth. Empowerment, after all, is not a static end-goal, but rather an ongoing and dynamic process of self-discovery, growth, and transformation. It is crucial to surround ourselves and our descendants with an infrastructure of care and support, that enables this unbridled potential to flourish.

Within our communities, we must dedicate ourselves to fostering mentorship relationships that span intergenerational gaps, nurturing the budding ambitions of young Black girls who will one day lead the way as brilliant scholars, pioneering scientists, and unparalleled artists. Our endeavors to provide guidance, resources, and opportunities tailored to the unique aspirations and talents of these girls will serve as crucial stepping stones for them to tread upon as they ascend to new heights of achievement.

Moreover, we must also emphasize the absolute necessity of solidarity, sisterhood, and empathy among ourselves as a community. Recognizing and appreciating the power of our shared experiences serves as a vital foundation that allows us to uplift one another on our collective journey of empowerment. In the proud tradition of our ancestors, we must continue to weave together our stories, dreams, and potentials into a dazzling quilt of resilience, igniting a beacon of inspiration, empowerment, and hope that stretches far into the distant horizon.

In the fullness of time, as the winds of change continue to sweep through our world, let us not lose sight of the shimmering constellation of potential that illuminates our hearts, minds, and spirits. As we gather our dreams within our hands, we know that the visages of our ancestors smile upon us, and the echoes of their resilience resound within our very souls. The boundless potential of Black women and their descendants is a living monument to their strength and courage, a testament to the eternal fire of hope that shall continue to burn brightly, guiding us forward towards a limitless future filled with possibility, progress, and the promise of a better world.

Reflecting on Resilience: The Unbreakable Spirit of Black Women

As we delve into the rich and multifaceted history of Black women, it becomes apparent that there is a recurring theme throughout the ages—an unyielding resilience and strength that has been passed down through generations, empowering these women to overcome adversity and soar to unimaginable heights. The journey of Black women has been a tapestry, woven with threads of hardship and threads of triumph, each strand stitched together with determination and unwavering persistence. As we embark on an exploration of the various milestones, it is crucial for us to pause and reflect, recognizing and honoring the profound resilience and strength that has characterized our remarkable narrative.

In the earliest records of human history, we find evidence of powerful African matriarchs who assumed positions of stature and leadership within their societies. From the enigmatic Queen Hatshepsut, who ruled Egypt with a firm hand and a legacy of prosperity, to the fierce Queen Nzinga, who valiantly defended her kingdom's sovereignty, these trailblazing women laid the foundations for a long lineage of female leaders who would follow in their footsteps. In reflecting upon their accomplishments, we are reminded of the innate ability of Black women to navigate and mold the course of their destinies, even in the face of seemingly insurmountable odds.

The resilience and strength of Black women became particularly crucial during the harrowing era of the transatlantic slave trade, a period that violently ruptured African societies and forcibly displaced millions of individuals. Amidst the horror and anguish of the Middle Passage and the brutal conditions of enslavement, Black women found solace and sustenance in the communities they forged among their fellow captives. Through shared experiences of pain and resilience, they developed intricate networks of support, allowing them to preserve not only their own spirits but to uplift one another.

Black women in this dark period laid the groundwork for the strong resistance that would define the centuries to come. Their acts of defiance took myriad forms, from quiet subversion and sabotage to bold and daring escapes. It was this unyielding spirit of resistance, fueled by an indomitable will to survive and a fierce determination to reclaim their freedom, which would inform the ethos of Black women's activism in later generations.

As the years progressed, and the tides of history shifted, Black women continued to showcase their resilience and strength, mobilizing for change during the Civil Rights Movement of the 1960s. Women like Rosa Parks and Fannie Lou Hamer took a stand against the oppressive Jim Crow laws of the time, asserting their humanity in the face of relentless prejudice, bigotry, and violence. These women's courage and fortitude can be considered emblematic of the resolve that lives on in the hearts of countless others who fought for justice.

The legacy of resilience and strength demonstrated by Black women throughout history extends beyond the realm of politics and activism, as they continued to break down barriers across various fields. In the sciences, we witnessed iconic trailblazers like Dr. Mae Jemison, who defied societal expectations to attain the prestigious title of the first Black woman astronaut. Black women have also proven their undeniable prowess in the arts, as evidenced by the works of luminaries such as Maya Angelou and Toni Morrison, whose literary mastery has transcended the confines of race and time to enrich the lives of readers across generations.

However, as we pause to reflect on the strength and resilience of Black women from various epochs, it is crucial that we not only marvel at their uncompromising determination but also take time to celebrate the unsung heroines whose quieter acts of bravery and perseverance may have gone unnoticed in the annals of history. Behind every well-known figure, there exists a multitude of nameless faces, the everyday mothers, daughters, and sisters who fought in countless untold battles against injustice, inequality, and despair. It is these women, in their tenacious pursuit of a better world and unwavering stand against adversity, who truly embody the resplendent spirit of endurance and fortitude that runs deep in the veins of Black women.

As we turn our gaze towards the future, it is vital that we stand firmly rooted in the knowledge of our history and the undeniable resilience and strength demonstrated by our ancestors. Each new generation of Black women is an echo of the trials, triumphs, and indomitable spirit that has defined our journey thus far, and it is through the wisdom of our foremothers that we continue to forge our own paths towards a world of hope, promise, and boundless potential. We must use this reflection to kindle the flames of our imaginations, invoking the strength of the past as a catalyst for innovation, growth, and progress in the present day.

As Octavia Butler, the visionary writer, once proclaimed, "Kindness eases change, love quiets fear." It is with this loving awareness of resilience and strength passed down through generations of Black women that we shall continue to extend our roots deep into the rich soil of our past, and from the nourishment of our ancestors' wisdom, we will richly bloom into our present and future callings. For it is only by recognizing the strength that has carried us thus far that we will be able to bridge the gap, forging the foundations for the generations to come, heralding a future brimming with possibility and limitless potential.

Unlocking Potential: The Role of Support in Fostering Success

The vital role of education in emancipating and empowering Black women cannot be understated. From the early days of clandestine gatherings held by enslaved women, desperate to attain the forbidden knowledge of reading and writing, to the determined scholars who braved the hostility of segregated schools in the twentieth century, the pursuit of education has long been synonymous with the pursuit of freedom for Black women. Indeed, it is through education that Black women have acquired the knowledge and skills needed to challenge the status quo, becoming powerful advocates for change in their communities and within society at large.

Take, for instance, the story of Mary McLeod Bethune, an educator and civil rights activist who devoted her life to providing educational opportunities for Black children, ultimately earning national recognition for her work and becoming a prominent leader in the fight for civil rights. In founding the Daytona Literary and Industrial Training School for Negro Girls in 1904, Bethune transformed the lives of countless young Black women and laid the groundwork for broader conversations around access to education in the United States. Throughout her life, she remained dedicated to promoting education as the key to a more liberated and empowered future for Black women and their descendants.

As such, it is imperative that we continue to advocate for equal opportunities for Black women in the realm of education, striving to break down systemic barriers and promoting policies that facilitate access to quality schooling for all. This involves not only addressing the institutionalized racism that can pervade public education, but also addressing the unique experiences and struggles that Black girls face as a result of intersecting forms of discrimination. By fostering a more inclusive educational environment, we create a world where Black girls are better equipped to embrace their potential and leave their indelible mark on history.

Similarly, the process of empowerment is a crucial component to unlocking the potential of Black women and their descendants. Empowerment is not simply about gaining power and control over one's own life, but about fostering a sense of self-worth and instilling the belief that one's dreams are achievable, no matter the obstacles in one's path. This involves promoting positive self-image, encouraging exploration and expression of one's own identity, and nurturing the growth of self-confidence and self-esteem.

This process can be facilitated through the intentional creation of spaces and programs designed to promote empowerment, such as mentorship initiatives and workshops that focus on building self-confidence and leadership skills. Through these avenues, Black girls and women have the opportunity to connect with role models who can provide guidance, inspiration, and encouragement, showing them that they, too, can achieve success and greatness. By forging these connections and nurturing a sense of belonging and self-confidence, we can ignite the flame of empowerment within the hearts of Black women, fueling their drive to pursue their dreams and fully embrace their potential.

The role of support in unlocking opportunities for Black women and their descendants cannot be overstated. As the saying goes, "it takes a village to raise a child," and this sentiment rings particularly true in the context of supporting the growth and development of Black girls. By building solid support systems through families, communities, and mentorship programs, we can create an infrastructure of care and encouragement that enables the potential of Black women to flourish.

Moreover, we must emphasize the importance of solidarity and sisterhood among ourselves and our communities, recognizing and appreciating the power of shared experiences as a vital foundation for mutual support and empowerment. In the proud tradition of our ancestors, we must continue to weave together our stories, dreams, and potentials into a dazzling quilt of resilience, igniting a beacon of inspiration, empowerment, and hope that stretches far into the distant horizon.

In conclusion, as new generations of Black women take the stage and continue the remarkable legacy of their foremothers, it is our responsibility as a society to safeguard their access to opportunities and uplift their journeys. By embracing the limitless potential of Black women and their descendants through the ongoing cultivation of education, empowerment, and support, we can ensure that their flames of ambition continue burning brightly, lighting the path towards a limitless future filled with possibility, progress, and promise. By taking on this mantle as guardians and torchbearers, we pave the way for a world in which the collective greatness of Black women can be harnessed and amplified, shaping a new narrative of hope, determination, and transcendent excellence.

Intergenerational Wisdom: The Gifts of Our Ancestors

Weaving together the vast tapestry of Black women's history, counting thread by thread, one cannot help but realize the integral role of intergenerational connections in shaping the narratives of power, resilience, and growth within the African diaspora. For it is through the sharing of age-old wisdom passed down from ancestors to descendants that both a sense of identity and a connection to the past are solidified, ultimately providing nourishment for the souls of future generations, who, in turn, carry the baton forward on the long bent path of progress and change.

As we tour the rich realms of Black women's history, we find countless instances of cultural, artistic, and spiritual traditions seeping into the heart and soul of myriad generations, only to be passed down under the warmth of the technological sun of innovation. A notable example of this legacy can be found in the West African art of storytelling, where griots, or oral historians, preserved history and values through the spoken word, enchanting listeners with tales of ancient heroes and heroines. In the African American tradition, this practice is echoed in the lore shared through storytelling quilts, where each intricate pattern imbibes a distinct message, narrative, or memory richly woven into the family's history.

In similar reverence of ancestral wisdom, tangible efforts have been made in recent years to preserve and celebrate the unique cultural heritage of the African diaspora. One such initiative is the Black Girl Magic movement, which focuses on promoting self-love and pride in Afro-textured hair, emphasizing the importance of embracing ancestral links to one's natural beauty. By instilling a sense of connection to the past and appreciation for the diverse array of hair textures within the Black community, this movement empowers future generations to challenge societal norms and embrace the legacy passed down from their ancestors.

In addition to nurturing the roots of identity through the celebration of cultural heritage, intergenerational connections also yield invaluable guidance in the forms of mentorship and educational initiatives rooted in historic struggles and lessons. Take, for instance, the Freedom Schools established by the Civil Rights Movement, which sought to teach Black children about their history, culture, and the nonviolent strategies employed by their foremothers and forefathers. Today's after-school programs and academic organizations echo this fundamental commitment to imparting ancestral knowledge, fostering an environment where young Black scholars can learn about their history, explore their identity, and glean wisdom from the struggles and triumphs of their predecessors.

Indeed, it is through these educational initiatives that the intellectual fruits of past generations nourish the growth of the sapling scholars, who, in turn, continue the cycle of progress by reaching down and passing on their own wisdom to those who come after them, thus maintaining the upward spiral of development and change. For it is by fostering a continuous flow of knowledge between the generations that the tree of the Black community finds rooted sustenance and bears the fruit of empowerment.

The impact of intergenerational connections extends beyond the realm of education, with threads of mentorship and support forming a vital lifeline for Black women navigating the ever-shifting waves of life's travails. Whether they exist as quiet whispers of encouragement, steadfast hands of guidance, or sturdy shoulders to lean on, these connections provide an invaluable safety net through the trials, triumphs, and tribulations of life, with each generation enriched by the wisdom and strength of the one before.

As we move towards the shores of the illimitable horizon of the future, let us not forget the resilience and vigor that flows through our veins, gifted to us by our ancestors who fought valiantly for the right to pass on their legacies to the generations that would follow. In the rich glow of this ancestral flame, we must seize the opportunity to cultivate, cherish and celebrate the intergenerational connections that link the paths of our past to the dreams and potentials of our future.

By harnessing these strands of ancestral wisdom and nourishing the unassailable ties between generations, we ignite the sparks that will lead to an illuminating bonfire, bathing future generations of Black women in a warm, resplendent glow, as they continue to bend the arc of their narratives towards justice, empowerment, and progress. It is within this radiant illumination that we may gaze downward and find our ancestors, their hands entwined with our own, cheering us on as we depart from the shadows and step boldly into the limitless expanse of the future.

Leading from Every Angle: Black Women as Multidimensional Leaders

As we soar upwards on the rising thermals of history, tracing the arc of Black women's journey towards self-actualization and fulfillment, we can behold a rich panorama of stories, each marked by a unique confluence of passion, ambition, and resilience. In every epoch, visionary Black women have challenged and transcended the boundaries of expectation, illuminating the expanse of human potential with their radiant courage and unwavering persistence in the face of adversity. It is these women who have played an integral role not only as trailblazers in their respective fields, but as architects of our collective future, shaping the course of human culture and progress as they etch their indelible marks into the annals of time.

In the realm of science, we find pioneers such as Dr. Mae Jemison, an accomplished physician and engineer who propelled herself into history as the first Black woman astronaut to travel into space. With her nimble hands deftly manipulating the levers of destiny, Jemison tore through the fabric of our cosmic limitations, planting seeds of inspiration for generations of Black women to follow. Today, a new crop of women scientists, such as Dr. Kizzmekia Corbett, the leading immunologist responsible for the development of Moderna's COVID-19 vaccine, continue to push the boundaries of discovery, armed with the determination, intellect, and resourcefulness borne from the legacy of their predecessors.

The world of politics and activism has seen no shortage of visionary Black women leaders who have channeled their convictions and passions into creating palpable change within their communities. The indomitable Shirley Chisholm, unflinching in the face of obstacles and adversity, shattered glass ceilings as the first African American woman elected to Congress in 1968, and by running as a 1972 presidential candidate, she forged a path for future generations of women politicians to follow. Today, the power and grace of Shirley Chisholm's legacy is exemplified by leaders such as Vice President Kamala Harris,

Congresswoman Ayanna Pressley, and Stacey Abrams, each of whom wield their influence to craft a more just and equitable society.

In the idyllic pastures of literature and the arts, Black women have honed their creative talents and unique voices to express the vibrant tapestry of their experiences, crafting enduring narratives that challenge convention and transform the world. Toni Morrison, the Nobel and Pulitzer Prize-winning novelist, spun intricate webs of prose to skillfully examine the complex facets of Black womanhood. That artistic spirit endures in the contemporary works of writers such as Chimamanda Ngozi Adichie, whose novels and essays give voice to multicultural and feminist perspectives, and Roxane Gay, whose unapologetic commentary on race and gender pushes boundaries and invites dialogue.

Beyond these illustrious examples, countless Black women continue to break barriers and redefine the limits of the possible within their chosen fields, from sports to technology and beyond. Today, as more Black women embrace their power and excel in their pursuits, their collective achievements lay the foundation for future generations to build upon the legacy forged by their foremothers.

As the horizon beckons and the future unfolds, it is our shared responsibility to uplift and empower the voices of Black women, ensuring that their talents, insights, and creative energies can infuse and enliven the tapestry of human civilization. We must continue to foster an environment in which the dreams and aspirations of Black girls are nurtured and celebrated, allowing their latent seeds of potential to sprout and blossom.

It is within this fertile ground, watered by the wisdom and resilience of ancestral roots and nourished by the sunlight of unyielding determination, that the next crop of visionaries and change-makers will emerge, poised to soar into the limitless cosmos of the future. Their voices, when joined in harmonious chorus, will reverberate through the vast expanse of time and space, calling forth a new dawn of innovation, creativity, and progress, as each generation breathes life into the dreams of the one before, bending the arc of their collective narratives towards justice, empowerment, and triumph.

Sisterhood Stronger Together: Fostering Connections for a United Future

In the symphony of humanity, the harmonics of sisterhood and solidarity among Black women reverberate with a resonance that binds hearts, enriches lives, and amplifies the collective strength of a unified community. As each vibrant note weaves together a rich and powerful tapestry of shared experiences, dreams, and aspirations, it becomes evident that fostering these connections is vital for perpetuating the unyielding resilience embodied by generations of Black women.

Sisterhood, in its purest form, transcends the constraints of mere blood ties and embraces the kinship that exists between souls who share a common heritage, bound together by the invisible threads of understanding, compassion, and empathy. It is within the nurturing embrace of sisterhood that Black women can find solace and support amidst the tempest of adversity that often accompanies their journey through life. Strength harvested from the depths of this camaraderie enables them to confront the challenges that they face with a resilience buoyed by the knowledge that they are not alone in their struggles.

Moreover, solidarity is the lifeblood that sustains and enriches the bonds of sisterhood, infusing them with a sense of shared purpose and common identity. Working together in unison, Black women are able to tackle the entrenched barriers of discrimination, prejudice, and marginalization, transforming these seemingly insurmountable obstacles into stepping stones on the path to empowerment and liberation. It is this spirit of solidarity that draws from the wellspring of ancestral resilience, channeling the fortitude and courage of generations past to fortify the resolve of the present and galvanize the dreams of the future.

One such vivid illustration of Black women fostering sisterhood and solidarity can be found in the formation of communal groups, such as book clubs, mentorship programs, or neighborhood alliances that offer spaces for robust and open conversations on the trials, tribulations, and triumphs unique to the Black female experience. Within these sanctuaries, the healing balm of empathy meets the electric spark of inspiration, as every shared story or spoken word imbues the soul with the knowledge that there exists a kinship that transcends time and space.

Technology, too, has lent its voice to the chorus of sisterhood and solidarity, with digital platforms providing Black women the means to transcend the geographical constraints of the physical realm. Through social media, networking websites, and online forums, Black women from across the globe can cultivate connections that deepen their understanding of diverse perspectives and experiences, collectively nurturing a global community of affirmation and support.

In the context of activism and advocacy, Black women are increasingly banding together, wielding the strength of sisterhood and solidarity as a catalyst for change. By forming alliances such as the Black Lives Matter movement, led by three Black women, Patrisse Khan-Cullors, Alicia Garza, and Opal Tometi, they are able to use their collective voice to advocate for justice, equity, and recognition, resolute in their efforts to remake the world in the image of their dreams.

In sustaining and celebrating the powerful legacy of Black women, fostering sisterhood and solidarity is as much an act of love as it is a commitment to a brighter and more dignified future. By cherishing the bonds that span oceans, generations, and lifetimes, Black women are able to draw from a font of resilience, wisdom, and courage inherited from their ancestors, using these fortifying tools to hone their skills and talents while bearing the mantle of integrity, dignity, and pride.

As we forge ahead into the uncertain frontiers of the future, let us embrace the bonds of sisterhood and solidarity with renewed vigor and dedication. For it is within these nurturing folds that we weave together the threads of our intertwined destinies, constructing an indomitable fortress of strength and resilience that shall steadfastly endure the winds of time.

From the charged particles of shared aspirations, experiences, and dreams, a radiant constellation of sisterhood and solidarity emerges, twinkling with the promise of a stronger, united future. Each shining point of light forms a guiding star, leading the way as we traverse the vast expanse of the cosmos, trailblazing our path through the stardust of history to alight upon the shores of a more equitable and empowered world, where the dreams and hopes of our ancestors find resplendent fulfillment in the limitless potential of our descendants.